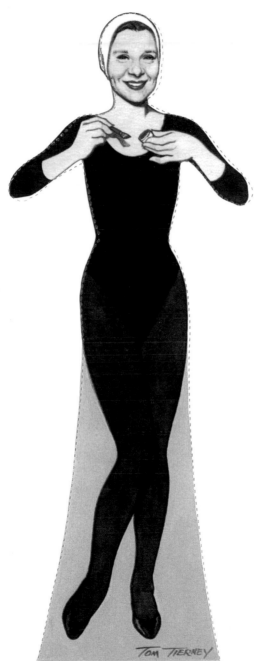

TRACEY
TAKES ON

TRACEY
TAKES ON

TRACEY ULLMAN

NEW YORK

Library of Congress Cataloging-in-Publication Data
Ullman, Tracey.
Tracey takes on / Tracey Ullman.
p.   cm.
ISBN 0-7868-6340-4
1. American wit and humor. I. Title.
PN6162.U45   1998
818'.5402–dc21   97-36648
CIP

PHOTO CREDITS: *Jim Britt/HBO*—pp. xxii (top), 72, 90, 95, 123, 139, 201; *Courtesy of Seymour Cassel*—p. 146; *Doug Hyun/HBO*—pp. xxi (bottom), xxiii (bottom), xxv (top), 21, 32 (top), 36, 62, 78, 86, 106, 136, 142, 166, 182, 189; *Roddy McDowell*—p. 96; *Tracy McLaughlin*—pp. 3, 4, 116, 117; *Terry O'Neill*—p. 22; *Matthew Rolston/Courtesy Fahey Klein, Los Angeles*—p. 178; *Martha Swope © Time Inc.*—p. 194; *Randy Tepper/HBO*—pp. xix, xx, xxi (top), xxiii (top), xxiv, xxv (bottom), xxvi, 11, 14, 15 (top), 20, 25-27, 38, 57-60, 68, 73, 76, 77, 87, 88, 93, 99, 102, 104, 105, 108, 113, 114, 126, 131, 133, 135, 148, 152, 153, 155, 163, 169, 170, 171, 181, 183, 184, 193, 197, 198, 200, 202-204, 205 (bottom), 206; *Courtesy of Twentieth Century Fox Television*—p. xiv (top); *Janet Van Ham/HBO*—pp. xxii (bottom), 35, 65, 92

All others: *Takes On Productions*

Designed by Robert Bull Design

FIRST EDITION

2 4 6 8 10 9 7 5 3 1

To Allan, Mabel, and Johnny, who know the real me.

ACKNOWLEDGMENTS

I would like to thank all the writers on the show: Jerry Belson, Dick Clement, Kim Fuller, Robert Klane, Jenji Kohan, Ian La Frenais, Molly Newman, Gail Parent, Tony Sheehan, and Allen J. Zipper.

I would further like to extend my gratitude to Jeff Bewkes, Chris Albrecht, and Carolyn Strauss at HBO, to Allan McKeown, our executive producer, and to the *Takes On* production staff, crew, and guest stars. These people make the show possible. Special thanks to Sam Clement.

CONTENTS

INTRODUCTION

FIVE YEARS AGO my husband, Allan, was bidding for a television franchise in the south of England, and he had to compile a programming schedule that he would implement if successful in his bid. Well, he put down the usual pie-in-the-sky shows that look good to judging panels: more local news (stories about cats up trees), intelligent children's programming (patronizing actors reading stories to sedated multiracial kids), sitcoms for the deaf, etc., etc. He told me that among this menu he had included a Tracey Ullman special. Thinking nothing would come of it, I continued nursing my newborn son, quite content to stay at home and wait for Woody Allen or Jane Campion to bring me out of an early retirement.

Then, in the middle of the night in September of '91, Allan called me. "We're winners, baby!" he exclaimed. "Oh, no!" I said. "I'll have to do that show now." I really was not prepared to do TV again. I had had an extraordinary run at Fox in the late '80s with the Tracey Ullman Show, and I couldn't imagine putting forth that amount of energy again. It had been a variety show that I performed weekly in front of a studio audience. Every show was different, I repeated some characters during the season, but not on a regular basis. The type of makeups I liked to disguise myself under had not been conducive to a live show—it had been crazy, with me running up and down stairs in between skits, ripping off rubber masks, and dousing myself in chemicals to dissolve all the glue. Once I inhaled so much remover that I passed out on the makeup room floor. I was resuscitated and went out to give a terrific performance, even though I can't remember being there.

So I had to think of a format for myself that would enable me to repeat characters and have time to apply my chins, lips, noses, teeth, mustaches, genitalia, etc., etc. I had a year to deliver the show, so I didn't panic, but while I read *Pat the Bunny* to Johnny and pushed him through plastic tubes at Tumble Time, I was gearing up to return to work.

A New ITV Comedy Special

Tracey Ullman
A CLASS ACT

MERIDIAN

SelecTV

I knew I was ready when one day I came upon a box of my wigs from the old show. I took each one out fondly and stroked them like cats. "Hello, Kay, how have you been?" I enquired of one. "Mustn't crumble, Tracey," she said, "but I'm tired of being in this box!" I soon found out that they all had a similar gripe, and as I was assuring them that they would soon be back in action, I realised that my daughter Mabel had come into the room and was watching me. "You're bloody nuts," she said. "Go back to work, this is pathetic!"

Michael Palin and myself in "A Class Act" (January 1993).

The special for Allan's TV station turned out to be "Tracey Ullman—A Class Act." It was a study of the English class system, and it was a great success. Having a rallying theme gave the show focus, and as it was filmed on location, I had plenty of time to apply the makeups.

Trevor Ayliss, my gay air steward, was created for this show. The makeup was extensive—a complete prosthetic face mask that gave me a manly brow, a square jaw, and a Kirk Douglas–like cleft in my fleshy chin. With a mustache, sideburns, and highlighted blow-dried hair, I was unrecognisable, until my baby Johnny arrived on the set. "Mama!" he cried from 40 feet away. How he knew it was me, mystifies me to this day. Both my children are very accepting of my work appearance; not many kids' mums dress up for a living as a hairy Middle Eastern cabbie or a seventy-year-old alcoholic with breasts down to her waist.

HBO became interested at this point and wanted me to take on a more American subject. So I chose New York, a character in itself.

Here I am, attacking Bart Simpson with my Emmy.

"Takes On New York" was filmed in three weeks, on location in Manhattan. I got to ride a police horse through Central Park and introduce Fern Rosenthal, my flame-headed Long Island housewife. I had seen this kind of woman many times in New York over the years. Loud, emotional, with "I'm from the suburbs" written all over her. She had sat behind me at matinees of *Cats* and *Les Miserables*, not too shy to shout out to the performers, "Speak up darling, we can't hear you!"

I loved being Fern, it was horrifying how naturally it came to me to wear shoulder pads, acrylic nails, and Windsong perfume on a semipermanent basis. I toyed with the idea of giving her her own series, but the emotional energy it took to be her left me like a limp rag, and my husband avoided me like the plague.

"Takes On New York" proved very successful too. I was now truly back into my schizophrenic, eclectic world, and very happy when HBO asked us to do a Takes On series. We set up production in Los Angeles in 1995. My husband, Allan, who co-produces the show with me, takes care of the business side of things and occasionally does on-camera work, playing the henpecked husband; but he tends to turn red and stare at the camera like a deer caught in the headlights, so I don't encourage it too much. I am head writer and work with a very talented group of people. In this capacity I adopt a Julie Andrews/ sheepdog persona, rounding up stray writers who are notorious for wandering off to make phone calls or to look for vast quantities of sugar to consume to make them "feel funny."

As I write this, we are starting production on our third season. I am enjoying it all immensely. Johnny is five and already a gifted mimic; Mabel rolls her eyes at my antics and tells me not to do my voices around her school friends. "I know it makes you happy, Mummy, but just control yourself." Allan's golf handicap is a frustrating 11, and he never did make that sitcom for the deaf.

CHARACTER BIOGRAPHIES

Trevor Ayliss – Age 43. An airline steward, based out of Heathrow, London, a short hop from his converted carriage house in Osterley, which he lovingly restored with his significant other, Barry, an antiquarian bookseller. Trevor enjoys amateur dramatics, line dancing, and Greco-Roman wrestling. He has been all over the world, but his favourite destinations remain Amsterdam, San Francisco, and the Greek island of Mykonos.

Virginia Bugge – Age 36. Virginia's husband is The Right Honourable Timothy Bugge, M.P. for Greater Diddlesbury. They have two children, Tamsin and Piers, who have attended boarding school since the age of six, leaving Virginia free to pursue her interests, which include fox hunting, grouse shooting, and bottling rhubarb chutney for the village fête.

Chic — New York City cabbie and "Chic Magnet" (hence the name) of indeterminate Middle Eastern origin. Chic is very single and was educated at "The University of Life, my friend!" Bronze-medal winner at the Pan Mediterranean Song Festival with his band Teiku, for their song "Slide Down My Olive Tree (Ooh Baby La La La)."

Kay Clark — Age 42. Bank teller and caregiver. Kay is from England but took a work transfer to California, to take advantage of American health care for her bedridden mother. Kay has never married. She did once bring a young man home, "but Mother rather spoiled it by staggering in, falling down in front of us, and screaming that she'd found something alive in her bedpan. It did rather blunt Cupid's arrow," chuckles Kay. "Still, mustn't crumble!" An eternal optimist, Kay keeps busy with her hobbies, which include cats (photographs only, Mother's allergic) and the collected works of the actor Harry Dean Stanton.

Hope Finch – Age 19. Hope is a student at Sweetbriar College and resides in the Margaret Sanger Hall. Although she hasn't declared a major yet, she is strongly considering Environmental Studies and Pre-Law, but only so she can devote herself to defending the poor and persecuted in a smoke-free atmosphere. She is not currently a lesbian, but she's young and impressionable.

Rayleen Gibson – Age 34. Stuntwoman. Rayleen hails from Australia, where until the age of ten, she was raised by dingoes, having been lost on a family camping trip as a tot. She grew up to become Hollywood's "Stuntwoman to the Stars" and now resides on a ranch, which she shares with her husband, Mitch, a little person, "but with a whanger like a king kangaroo!" and an assorted group of retired animal actors, including Sandy, the dog from the musical *Annie*, who was retired after he attacked his co-stars and still goes berserk when he sees anyone with red hair.

Birdie Godsen — Age 42. Devout Christian. Married to Bob, a tobacco industry executive. They live on Dan Quayle Drive within a graceful, gated, guarded community with their seven home-schooled children.

Linda Granger — Age (it varies). Seasoned performer, best known for her hit '70s TV series, *VIP Lounge*. Linda has inspired millions with her book *I'm Still Here! My Lifelong Battle with Alcoholism, Disease and Personal Misfortune . . .*, which she hopes to turn into a musical. Her closest allies are her agent, Candy Casino, and her "solid homosexual fan base." Linda lives in the Hollywood Hills with her teacup Pomeranian, Killer.

H.R.H.—Age 57. She has two birthdays: the day she was born, and her official birthday —a day that allows her subjects to rejoice. She has been very active recently in raising funds for a new Royal Yacht, something she believes is awfully important to the man in the street, "Even though he will never be allowed to set foot in it." Please send much needed contributions to any one of the fourteen Royal Houses, or contact www.HRH.commoners.

Sydney Kross—Age not available (it's illegal to ask that question). Beverly Hills attorney, a relentlessly ambitious and charmless litigator. Sydney is single, and was voted "The Girl You'd Least Like to Have a Blow Job By" in law school. Her motto is "You name it, I'll sue it!"

Erin McColl — Age 47. Former lead singer of the '70s supergroup Wisechild. Erin suffered what was described as "severe cerebral feedback" after the famous ale spiking incident at the Nebworth Festival. But with a program of herbal elixirs, colonic irrigation, and crystal absorption, she is making a steady comeback at Classic Rock Expos and Pro-Choice rallies. She is guided by her faithful manager/earth mother/nursemaid, Dusty Roads.

Mrs. Noh Nang Ning — Age 70. Donut shop owner of indeterminate Asian origin. A hardworking patriotic American, she finds that most of life's events bear direct analogies to the humble donut — "The circle of life!" Madam N works long hours, finding little time for pleasures such as sponsoring her niece in ice dance competitions and playing Paigow in Vegas.

Janie Pillsworth – Age 37. Magazine editor. Born Janine Pillsworth, in Broxbourne, England, the only child of Frank and Jackie, who sacrificed everything to send her to a private school (Frank even sold a kidney). Eventually she disowned her working-class parents and, armed with her new identity, swiftly rose up the publishing ladder to her present appointment – editor of *Manhattan Review Magazine* – whereupon an unscrupulous colleague revealed her true identity. A tearful reunion with her estranged parents ensued. Now her widowed mother, Jackie, conveniently works for Janie in her Upper East side apartment as a housekeeper/nanny. Janie has two children, Olivia and Daniel, with her husband Gregor, a university professor thirty years her senior.

Ruby Romaine – Age 72. A Hollywood makeup artiste. Ruby moved to Los Angeles at the age of fifteen with her son, Buddy, who found childhood fame as The Tasty Bread poster boy. She also has a daughter named Desirée from her short-lived marriage to the entertainer Tubby Lapels, chairman emeritus of the Hermosa Beach Friars Club. Ruby's hobbies are poker, wine tasting, and preserving the old Hollywood, "so it don't turn into Boomshakalaka town."

Fern Rosenthal —Age 56, an energetic homemaker, formerly of Long Island, now living in Boca Raton, Florida. Fern's husband, Harry, is a retired pharmacist. They have one daughter named Sheila and a son-in-law known as "the putz." Fern's hobbies are shopping and the theater—she loved *Cats*. She is an active member of her condo board, and for the last two years has been the chairwoman of the "Temple of Israel of Boca Raton" Purim carnival. As Fern says, "I'm a giver, I love to give."

Chris Warner —Age 32. Life companion to Midge Dexter, a professional golfer. Chris and Midge lead an openly gay life, after their very public display of affection on the 18th green following Midge's victory at The Slimline Classic. Chris has put her career as a step aerobics teacher on hold in order to tour with Midge, acting as her spiritual adviser and nutritionist.

TRACEY
TAKES ON

CHAPTER
ONE
CHILDHOOD

TRACEY ULLMAN ON CHILDHOOD

I was never a child, I was always a menopausal woman in a child's body. Here I am when I was six years old; as you can see my mother had taken an unsuccessful chop at my bangs.

And here I am with some of the toys from my childhood. They're very personal and dear to me. The black-haired doll with the lopsided smile is Wendy Boston. When I first got her she had on a little pink bonnet, pink mittens, and a pink dress. But within twenty minutes I had stripped her naked and left her underneath the sprinklers in the front garden. The savaged gnome in the floppy hat is Mr. Rumble-belly, and he's from  Poland. Unfortunately my Yorkshire terrier Sooty, who we got from Harrods, no less, mauled him. That dog had no class.

I grew up in a rural area just outside London and rode ponies and took part in gymkhanas and made houses out of bales of hay in the cornfield at the end of my garden, and I could imitate anyone! The spinster who lived opposite us who wore rubber boots, and always had a "dewdrop" hanging from her nose, my Auntie Irene who was from Liverpool and chain smoked while knitting baby booties—it all came quite naturally to me.

My mother's family were all from South London, and they would visit us and tell my mum that her kids "talked posh," so I decided to adopt a Cockney accent, it sounded more definitive, rebellious, not so suburban: "Oy mush, wanna punch up the bracket?" Of course, when I rode my pony and mixed with the Volvo/lemon squash crowd, I put on my "Gosh, thanks awfully!" voice. And when my stepfather's gay cousin from Miami visited I learned to say, "Honey, get the hell outta here!" Who would have thought that I would grow up to make a living out of this parrot-like ability.

Here I am giving you an example of something else I liked to do as a child, only now that I'm grown up I know to wear panties.

H.R.H. ON CHILDHOOD

PIP

Your old governess, Your Highness.

H.R.H.

Oh, Nanny Blair, you're still alive. I remember when I was a little girl you made me join the local Brownie troupe because you thought that playing with the children of ordinary people would be a humbling experience for me. All I can say is that when they went home in their bad shoes to their little homes I felt terribly superior and awfully grateful that I lived in a castle. I expect you miss living in a castle, don't you? Are we still sending you the jar of grouse pâté on your birthday? Good.

Good-bye.

"EVERY DAY FRESH!!"

MRS. NOH NANG NING ON CHILDHOOD

MY CHILDHOOD BAD. VERY HARD. I WAS ORPHAN. PARENTS KILLED DURING BIG RIOT AT COCKFIGHT. THEY LAND IN MIDDLE OF RING, GET PECKED TO DEATH. SEE? THEY DIED IN MIDDLE OF BIG CIRCLE. YEAH. MY WHOLE LIFE ABOUT BIG CIRCLE, JUST LIKE DONUT!

RAYLEEN GIBSON ON CHILDHOOD

Here's a picture of me with my cousin Moishe, that's right, my cousin. I was raised by dingoes. I was lost on a family camping trip to the outback when I was just a tot. Yeah, there were too many kids in the family to miss just one. And I would have died if the dingoes hadn't taken me in and let me run with the pack. I loved the life. It was great living outdoors and I never had any trouble until I encountered my first *human* animal. I'd been living with the dingoes for about ten years. I traveled with them, slept with them, ate with them . . . even hunted with them. I could hold my own, too. I was as fast and agile as any of them, and a lot smarter, too, except this one night. . . .

We were out on our nightly roustabout when we came across a farm, and that meant chickens! I pried open the door of the barn with my hot little paw and we were in! Me and the rest of the family were so busy having our chicken smorgasbord that we never heard the farmer arrive with his shotgun. Moishe and the rest of the family managed to escape, only I was cornered. I suppose you could say I was caught chicken-handed. Although I don't know who was more surprised, me or that farmer. There was something about this bloke that reminded me of my own father . . . and since I could tell what a person was like just by smelling his ass, I gave him the once-over. I liked him! That night the farmer and his daughter took care of me. I slept by the fireside and dreamed of

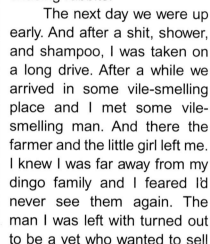

chasing rabbits.

The next day we were up early. And after a shit, shower, and shampoo, I was taken on a long drive. After a while we arrived in some vile-smelling place and I met some vile-smelling man. And there the farmer and the little girl left me. I knew I was far away from my dingo family and I feared I'd never see them again. The man I was left with turned out to be a vet who wanted to sell me to the circus. At the time all I knew was that his ass smelled like a dung beetle's breakfast! He threw me in a rusty pen in the back room with a bowl of slimy water and a pedigree turd on the floor that the last occupant had left me. I took comfort in humping a pillow— I missed my dingo boyfriend. Suddenly, I heard a meow, looked up, and saw a cat sitting on a ledge beneath a slightly opened window.

Now if there's one thing that got my goat, especially when I thought I was a dog, it was cats. I leaped up onto the ledge, just

missing that manky moggy, who took off out the window. I squeezed myself through, tumbled into the alley below, and was off in hot pursuit, barking my head off. Fluffy shot up a squiggly gum tree and onto a flat roof and I followed. We scrambled across the tiles making a huge ruckus until we ran out of roof. I had him! He cowered on the edge. I crept towards him, hackles raised, and let out a low growl from the back of my throat. But then the fearless feline jumped 50 feet into the alley below, and in the heat of the moment, I did too. I didn't know it at the time, but I'd just done my first triple-spin, rib-tucked half-twist body launch; a signature jump that I later used successfully in *French Connection II*. I landed on all fours, right in the path of an oncoming car, which screeched to a halt. "That was a great stunt! Ever thought about being in the movies?," shouted the driver. I looked at her, cocked

my head to one side, and something told me that this pretty blonde human would feed me, worm me, and scratch my tummy buttons.

And that's exactly what she did. She also let me howl along to her record "Have You Ever Been Mellow." The rest, as they say, is history. That tart in the car was kind enough to send me to school and see to my education and put me in touch with some film producers.

I've assimilated into the human race pretty well, but sometimes when I'm in the park with my husband, Mitch, and someone throws a ball, I still find myself chasing after it!

RUBY ROMAINE
ON CHILDHOOD

Ya know, I matured at a very early age. By the time I was ten years old, I had hair in all four locations — and bazongas like two torpedoes. I was a pretty little thing.

About that time my uncle Roscoe lost his job as a mule skinner and came to live with us. Yeah, he was very fond of me, Uncle Roscoe.

And then I got smart and I made a stink about a certain situation, and the judge made him join the Navy and they sent him to Guam. God rest his sweaty paws.

Anyhoo, some time later a major motion picture called <u>Pirate of the Plains</u> came to our town. And I caught the eye of the star, Mr. Errol Flynn.
He said I was "bewitching," and then he passed out on top of me. He

called me his little girl Friday . . . even though we did it on Mondays and Thursdays, too. And then I threatened to make a stink about his swordplay, if you get my drift. And he got me a job as a makeup girl. And that's how I started my career. Yeah, it was a good year. And then I turned fifteen. . . .

THE
GYPSY
CAB
COMPANY

CHIC ON CHILDHOOD

You want to know the greatest thrill of my childhood? Was when my family and I first sailed into New York Harbor — and I got my first glance at that Foxy Lady — The Statue of Liberty. Hey, she wasn't easy to see, I was stuffed in a barrel with my sister!

TREVOR AYLISS ON CHILDHOOD

I was brought up in the north of England that you only see in those black-and-white films. Factory chimneys, colliery wheels, terraced houses, and wet streets with women in head scarves pushing prams. Not the best place for a lad with my sensibilities. . . .

I remember I was twelve years old and still sharing a bedroom with my two brothers. I was forever picking up sweaty socks and athletic supports — that smell still sends a strange thrill through me. Anyhow, this particular Saturday, our local soccer team, Doncaster Rovers, was playing at home, and I was determined to get Dad to take me. I could hear him downstairs with my big brothers, supping tea and spitting on the fire. "Now don't let the lads drink too much, Geoffrey," came me mam's familiar cry. "They've got to learn, Elsie, they're six-teen," said Dad. "Well, just a couple of pints at halftime then."

I put on my freshly pressed gabardine raincoat, pinned a homemade rosette to my lapel, and ran down the stairs swinging my football rattle. "I'm ready, Dad!" I shouted. "Ready for what?" said my father, buttoning his coat and looking at me through his National Health glasses. "I heard you say you had a spare ticket." "I did," he said. "I gave it to Mr. Rowbotham's lad." I hung my head, feeling the familiar rejection. "Oh, he's disappointed, Geoffrey," said me mam. "You could take him. You've never taken him before." "I 'ave!" blustered me dad. "I took him when he was two, he cried through the whole bloody game! Anyhow, he doesn't like football, he wanted ice skates for his birthday!" I could hear my brothers sniggering, "Please, Dad." My father turned in the doorway.

"Son, it's a big match, there'll be a crush. . . .You're a delicate lad; it could bring on your asthma. You stay home with your mother. All right lads, let's go!" I felt a spiteful jab in the ribs and an elbow in the balls as a surge of manhood passed through our hallway. Then I felt a comforting hand on my shoulder and the familiar smell of lavender and lard, "I'm baking a cake, Trevor," Mam said. "You can help me ice it."

I felt a lot better and sat at our kitchen table in a clean apron squeezing blobs of fudge onto a victoria sponge. "That's lovely, our Trevor," Mam said. "They won't think so," I said pitifully. "They don't think I'm good at anything." "What do you mean by that?" "Well, me brothers both play football for the school. Me dad wins all those trophies with his racing pigeons. Even me sister won a beauty contest." Me mam tensed a little, "Only because she slept with the judges, pet." "I just feel different, Mother," I said. She sensed my despair, stopped slicing tripe and sat down beside me. She told me that I was different, I was artistic and sensitive, that's why I'd seen *Calamity Jane* at the Regal seven times, that's why I was good at embroidery and wanted an accordion. "You've got talent, our lad, and don't you forget it!" she said. I felt my spirits rise. She smiled. "I know how to cheer you up, our Trevor, come with me."

She took my hand and we went upstairs to her bedroom. I loved playing with my mam's things—all she had was a few pieces of paste jewelry, worn-down lipsticks, and a mangy old fox fur, but to me it was like stepping into Christian Dior's atelier. She put her rayon blouse with the Peter Pan collar on me and cinched in the waist with me dad's work belt. Then I put on her lambskin pixie boots with the Cuban heels and side zippers; a chiffon scarf tied jauntily round my neck completed the look. I was Doris Day! Ready to ride on the Deadwood Stage. We rehearsed all afternoon. We made a whip out of a wooden spoon and some clothesline. Over and over, I perfected my routine, until we heard the men arriving home.

"Bloody ref, wants his eyes tested," I heard my dad muttering. The others mumbled in agreement as they hung up their coats in the hallway. Our team had lost by the sound of it. Well, I knew just how to cheer them up! My mam met them in the front parlour, and I heard her say, "I've got a lovely surprise for you men. Trevor's going to put on a little show for you." "What's this? What's this? Not another bloody magic show like last Christmas, I was right fond of those bloody goldfish," grumbled me dad. "Oh, shut up, Geoffrey, and take your seat!" I trembled with anticipation against the kitchen wall. I heard the needle placed on the well-worn record. I poked my head round the door and Mam gave me an enthusiastic thumbs-up. It was Show Time! Slapping the whip to my rump I trotted in, head held high.

Oh, the Deadwood Stage is rolling on over the plains!
With the curtains flappin' and the driver slappin' the reins!

Out of the corner of my eye I could see them all lined up watching me—I had their complete attention. I stopped and faced them in a classic Doris stance, one hand on my hip, one shading my eyes from the blazing sun,

Beautiful sky, a wonderful day—so!
Whipcrackaway! Whipcrackaway! Whipcrackaway!

With each Whipcrack-away I flicked the wooden spoon and stamped my pixie boots. Their mouths were open in admiration. Mam tapped her toe and mouthed the words along with me. Growing more confident I sauntered over to Mr. Row-botham and perched on his knee,

We're headed straight for town, loaded down,
with some fancy cargo . . .

I tried to ruffle his hair, but my fingers got stuck in hair oil.

Care of Wells and Fargo, Illinois . . .

As I mouthed "Boy!" and did a perky pirouette around the coal scuttle, the music stopped and the needle was abruptly dragged back to its station. I turned to see my dad standing grim-faced by the gramophone. There was a moment of silence that was broken by Mr. Rowbotham getting to his feet and telling his son to fetch his coat. Before he left, he leaned in to my father and said in a low, angry voice, "He's not *my* son, Geoffrey, but if he were, I'd thrash him till he bleeds."

I didn't understand, my head was pounding. I stared at my mam, who looked as confused as I did. Before I burst into tears and got called a big Jessie, I ran to my room and lay there sobbing and pouring my heart out to my Eartha Kitt poster. Then I heard my father coming up the stairs. I dived under the bedspread in anticipation of a beating and stayed there whimpering until I heard him say, "It's all right, lad, I'm not going to hurt you." I peeked out and looked up at the hairs growing out

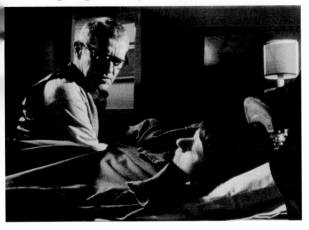

of his nostrils. "I want you to grow up to be a man, like your dad and all the other Aylisses before you. Work ten hours a day down the mine, have a bath once a week, get pissed on Saturdays, and die at forty of black lung disease. Now that's a man's life!"

My father passed on fifteen years ago now. He never could come to terms with my homosexuality. Unlike my mother, who's a very merry widow! She takes low-impact aerobic classes twice a week at the church hall, and last year Barry and I took her on a gay cruise, round the Florida Keys. I've got a cracking photo of her doing the Macarena with four boys in thongs! And being an air steward is a man's life! Canapes don't come on presauced, you know, and before they banned that in-flight smoking, I thought I was going to die from black lung disease. Oh, Wristflapaway, wristflapaway, wristflapaway!

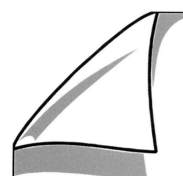

Wimpman, <u>KROSS</u>, and <u>Wussman</u>
"You name it, we'll sue it." *(Since 1987)*
PENTHOUSE
F. LEE BAILEY LEGAL CENTER
100 CANON DRIVE
BEVERLY HILLS

FROM THE COMMAND STATION OF SYDNEY KROSS

I know I'm a
little abrasive.
I have been since
I was a child.
When I was born,
the doctor slapped
me on the butt.
I later sued him for
sexual harassment.
I collected two
mill. I also sued
the hospital for
serving my Similac
too hot. I collected
three mill. And when
my mother refused to
breast-feed me — I sued for custody of her bosom.
I didn't win, but I got to visit them three times
a day. I sucked that bitch dry.

MANHATTAN REVIEW MAGAZINE

from the editor's desk...

JANIE PILLSWORTH ON CHILDHOOD

My childhood was incredibly safe, secure, and predictable. I cycled to school and tennis lessons without being shuttled or chaperoned. No one was vandalized, mugged, shot, or raped. No one's parents got divorced, nobody's priest molested choirboys.

One's elder brother wasn't a junkie and none of one's school chums suffered from depression, low self-esteem, or food disorders. That's why I've never written a book. I'd hate all this to come out in the sleeve notes. . . . ◆

CHAPTER
TWO
ROYALTY

TRACEY ULLMAN ON ROYALTY

Here I am in 1984, meeting Princess Diana at a charity rock concert. As you can see, like most people who do their hair at home, I had forgotten to comb the back. This meeting was filmed for the evening news, and my horrified mother called me and told me that my hair looked like a duck's arse!

Over the years my family has had a few more embarrassing incidents with royalty. My daughter Mabel met Princess Diana when she was five and held up the receiving line by asking Diana why she wasn't wearing a crown. "You don't look like a princess with short hair," she said. "It should be long, like the princesses in fairy tales." "Her Royal Highness really must move on now," said a lady in waiting, kindly. "But I haven't finished with her yet," said a disgruntled Mabel.

Then, in the summer of '96, when my son Johnny was four years old, we went to an open-air rock concert in Hyde Park, attended by H.R.H. Prince Charles. Our great friends Harvey and Diane Goldsmith had organised this event, and when we arrived straight from the airport after a long journey from Italy, they were very keen to present their godson Johnny to the Prince. Now Johnny's the kind of kid who, by three in the afternoon, is in a right state: hair sticking up, shirt hanging out, and if his hands touch you, you have to get a tetanus shot. Well, he was all of the above that day, plus he'd had a sticky ice pop on the Milan to Gatwick leg, which had made his hands particularly tactile. Before I could hose him down, Harvey and Diane whisked him off to meet the Prince. I stood back and watched Johnny be introduced to H.R.H., who was suitably dressed for a rock concert in a Savile Row suit. "Hello," he said, accepting Johnny's outstretched paw. "Hello," said Johnny. "I've just been on holiday."

At this point Prince Charles tried to extricate himself from Johnny's grasp, but had become stuck. "Have you been drinking Coca-Cola?" Johnny stared at him, his face covered in dust and felt marker, "Yeah, I'll have a Coke!"

We imagined that the next day the Prince summoned his equerry, wanting to know how he could get rid of a strange rash that had developed on his hand, "One feels one has been in contact with something quite alien." We look forward to our next close encounter.

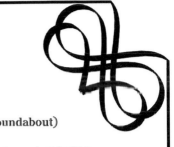

Trevor Ayliss
& Barrington LeTissier
Willows Mews Cottage
Osterly on the Green
Middlesex, MD12 6HE
(Come off the M40 at the Robin Hood Roundabout)

TREVOR AYLISS ON ROYALTY

I had a brush with royalty once. We had Barbara Cartland in First Cabin. She's brilliant. She dictated two new books and a short story to her assistant between New York and London. I was Johnny-on-the-spot with the teapot that night, so I could eavesdrop on the stories. It was marvellous. And do you know what happened? She named one of her characters Trevor! He was an Albanian duke in exile. I was ever so touched. Trevor was dark and brooding and had limpid blue eyes that could burn through you and make your heart race 'til you thought you'd swoon. He had broad shoulders and slim hips. He wore tight jodhpurs and riding boots, and his shirt often blew open to reveal his sinewy neck and tan muscular chest. And he had a poet's soul. He was beautiful. Ohhh, that Mrs. Cartland. She can see things other people can't.

RUBY ROMAINE ON ROYALTY

I'm going out with my boyfriend tonight. I guess you could say he's royalty in a manner of speaking. He's Mel Klipsch, the King of Water Heaters. Mel treats me pretty good. He always takes me out to dinner someplace. He's a nice lookin' fella and he's a snappy dresser. You know those doubleknit trousers that don't take a belt? He's got every color they make. And he's got a very expensive, custom-made toupee, although I pretend I don't notice. He's very generous, too. Last Christmas he gave me a 75-gallon hot water heater. I've been going out with Mel for a few years now. He's married, you know, but I like it that way. I wasn't cut out to be the Queen of Water Heaters. I don't need that kind of responsibility.

VAN NUYS SAVINGS & LOAN

KAY CLARK

ASSISTANT BRANCH MANAGER

KAY CLARK ON ROYALTY

That's one of the things Mother and me miss, living in America. A royal occasion. We used to love it when the Queen inspected her troops. And I tell you it can't be easy riding a horse sidesaddle. I said to Mother once, "Perhaps they Velcro her to the horse," but she thought I was being disloyal, got very upset, and coughed out her catheter.

But our favourite's the Queen Mother. Her husband only became king because his brother abdicated on account of that awful Mrs. Simpson woman. She cast some alluring spell over him, that's for sure. I can't see it myself. From the photographs she always looked slightly constipated. I expect that's why they sought exile in France—because of the suppositories.

We saw the Queen Mother once. She came to open a play-ground for Teenage Drug Addicts in Roehampton. That's where Mother and I were living at the time, about 200 yards from the Artificial Limb Fitting Center. Just in case, you know. . . .

Anyway, we were right by the entrance when she got out of the Daimler, wearing a powder blue two-piece. The mayor stepped forward in his chains of office and said, "Good morning, Your Majesty, what would you like to do first? See the geraniums or talk to some delinquents?" And the Queen Mother replied, with all the authority that comes with centuries of Sovereignty: "What we'll do first, you silly bugger, is have a very stiff gin and tonic."

We had a laugh, Mother and me. 'Course, laughing's not something Mother should do, medically speaking, so we ended up in an Intensive Care Unit. . . . Never mind. We had the memory, we had the day.

A LARK WITH KAY CLARK

YOU DON'T HAVE TO
BE CRAZY TO WORK
HERE, BUT IT HELPS!

HOUSE OF COMMONS

Timothy Bugge, M.P.

TIMMY and VIRGINIA BUGGE ON ROYALTY

When I got home that evening Virginia was reading the *Horse and Hound* with a pot of Earl Grey. I had just come back from Whitehall on the 5:22 express and was feeling rather pleased with myself. "Hullo! I'm home. . . ." Virginia, as usual, skipping the pleasantries, stayed silent, so I helped myself to a cup of tea. That's when she must have noticed my rather jolly mood.

"Why are you looking so pleased with yourself, Timmy?"

"Didn't know I was."

"You're smirking. Which means you think you've done something clever. Time to worry, in my experience."

"Well, you know I've been looking for a Royal to open the new Animal Husbandry Museum."

"I hope they haven't fobbed you off with Fergie."

"Bit higher up the tree than that, old girl."

"Duchess of Kent?"

I gestured higher yet.

"Not the Queen?"

"Not the Queen, no, but not a million miles from the Queen."

"Good Lord, Timmy, not . . . ?"

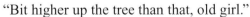

"Spot on," I said. "And as the sitting Member of Parliament I shall be expected, along with my good lady wife, to host a luncheon for said H.R.H."

"Oh, Timmy, you've been frightfully clever! I shall give you a good spanking and let you watch *Baywatch*."

"Both at the same time?" I gasped.

About two weeks later I was coming in from the garden when I saw Virginia with a young chap. He seemed to be in his early thirties. He had short hair, pink cheeks, and looked like he spent a lot of his spare time on a horse. I noticed that Virginia looked surprisingly deferential and was carrying a notebook and pencil. On my way over to introduce myself I overheard them. Virginia was talking about seating arrangements.

"This is the dining room. Ten, you said? That's no problem, we frequently seat thirty."

"There'll be Her Royal Highness, myself, and her private secretary. Apart from that, you can ask anyone who isn't boring. This carpet—pity about the colour."

"Really?"

"Not her favourite. H.R.H. only likes burgundy in a glass."

At that point the young chap, obviously some sort of royal adviser, lifted the corner of the carpet with his suede brogue.

"Tell you what. You've got a halfway decent bit of parquet under here. Get rid of the carpet and get a French polisher in."

Virginia was scribbling this down in her notebook as I introduced myself.

"Hul-lo!"

"Oh, Timmy, this is Captain Philip St. Aubyn, Equerry to H.R.H."
We shook hands.

"Call me Pip, please. Now, dogs. H.R.H. loves them, but not other people's. I noticed a Labrador in the garden," he said, nodding towards the lawn.

"That's Baxter, we've had him fourteen years."

"About time he was put down then. H.R.H. feels the same way about children. You unfortunately have some."

"Unfortunately we do," Virginia chirped.

"Do we have to have them put down?" I said, a little unsure.

"Timmy!"

"Heavens no. Just keep them well out of the way."

Virginia had arranged to send them to Scotland for the day, but said if that wasn't far enough she had a cousin in Oslo.

"Terrific. Great. I'll leave the menu to you, but she hates carrots and beet roots. And only English cheeses. White wine during lunch—something crisp, honeyed, and slightly musky. And please remember, no one must leave the room before H.R.H. No one must leave their chair before Ma'am does."

I asked what I thought was a rather warranted question. "Um . . . what if one wants to use the potty?"

"One waits," Pip replied rather sternly.

On the day of the visit there were police cars in the driveway and men in dark suits with walkie-talkies, strategically positioned on the lawn. I must admit that I was a little nervous, but it was very exciting all the same. In the dining room we'd had the parquet floor polished and had out the best crockery—a wedding gift from Mother. We'd invited some friends from the club to make up the numbers. H.R.H. sat at the head of the table, of course, and I was to her right. Virginia was at the other end and Pip, the only chap who seemed relaxed, was seated in the center. Jeffrey, the butler, and two maids were in attendance.

"One finds that one Royal Tour is much the same as another," Ma'am began. "One arrives, one speaks of the bond between our nations. One waves at flag-waving schoolchildren. And one accepts some indigenous gift, usually quite impractical, from a tribal elder." At that she poked at something on her plate. "Is this chicken?"

"It's pheasant, Ma'am," Virginia nervously volunteered.

"Really? So hard to tell under this dubious sauce." Not wanting to disagree with royalty, I conceded, "It is rather revolting, awfully sorry."

"Interesting wine, though."

"Thank you, Ma'am. Went to some trouble." And I had.

"It manages to be bland and acid both at the same time."

She pushed her plate away, put a cigarette in a holder, and held it to her lips. Virginia flashed me one of her looks . . . of course, I quickly picked up the lighter from the table, but the damn thing wouldn't catch. I was at a loss as to what to do. "Um, I do have a table lighter in the sideboard, Ma'am," I managed to say.

"If it were upon the table, you'd be able to light my cigarette," she said. Still a little unsure as to what to do, I looked over to Pip for some guidance on protocol. Thankfully he gave me the go ahead with a nod. I got up out of my chair to fetch the lighter.

"The most curious gift I ever received was in Fiji," continued H.R.H. "Or was it Tonga? Anyway, it was a pair of something strange in a camphor wood box."

Just then, as I was heading for the sideboard, I slipped on the newly polished floor, flew up into the air, and landed rather awkwardly on my arse, crushing my left arm. I couldn't help but cry out in pain. I was sure that it was broken, or at least badly fractured. There I was, helplessly writhing around in agony. The room was frozen for a moment. I noticed that people were looking in every strange direction, just not at me. Virginia risked a glance as I clutched my arm in pain. I saw her half rise and cautiously look towards Pip. He moved his head gravely from side to side and she sat back down. H.R.H. still held her unlit cigarette.

"Has anybody got a match?" Jeffrey leaped forward to offer her a light. I managed the best I could and crawled over to Virginia. "I think I've broken my arm!" I hissed.

"Quiet, Timmy, don't make a fuss."

"I can see the bone!"

Virginia pointedly ignored me. I can't say that I blamed her—I must have looked an awful sight. She turned to H.R.H. "The things in the wooden box, do tell, what were they, Ma'am?"

"A pair of marmosets' testicles pickled in brine. Some sort of healing properties supposedly. I pretended they were earrings and gave them to Fergie for Christmas, and every time I visited, she felt obliged to wear them."

She let out a delicate laugh, and everybody else chuckled dutifully.

"Why doesn't someone tell a joke?" she continued. "I love jokes, provided they make me laugh."

There was an awkward silence. I couldn't help muttering something about getting an ambulance. Virginia gave me a little kick.

"Timmy, you know a joke. Get up and tell it."

Virginia hauled me to my feet. My face must have been white with pain, as my broken arm hung uselessly at my side. I began to tell the joke through clenched teeth, "A Cardinal, an Archbishop, and a Rabbi were playing golf . . ."

"I do hope I haven't heard it," Ma'am said.

I struggled through the joke bravely but nonetheless seemed to fluff the punchline. I dragged myself back to my chair, and we soldiered on through the summer pudding. After we'd finished the cheeses and port, I could see the shadows darkening in the garden outside, I think that the strain of it all was even getting to Virginia. She had a glassy stare and a frozen smile on her face. I was slumped next to H.R.H., trying to stop my head from hitting the table. H.R.H. spoke.

"I do so miss amusing people. In the old days, I always had Peter Sellers or Sammy Davis Jr. to amuse me. Did you know him?" she said, turning to me. Then she gave me what I think was a playful prod. "Frightfully funny! What a hoot!"

With a supreme effort I managed to stay silent and conscious.

"Nowadays, everywhere I go I'm surrounded by bores."

Pip interjected. "Excuse me, Ma'am, but if you want to be home in time for the *X Files* . . . "

"Yes, I suppose we should be pushing off."

H.R.H. rose. Everyone else followed suit—but I couldn't.

"If you could point one towards the porcelain, I'll powder my nose." She then followed Pip out of the room, obviously not feeling the need to thank us —with lunch having been such a fiasco.

One of the guests asked if there was another loo. Virginia answered, "Up-stairs."

There was a stampede. Chairs knocked over, glasses broken. When it was just Virginia and me left at the table, she turned on me, "I've never been so mortified in all my life! You chose the wrong wine, you completely messed up your joke, and you didn't even rise when she left the room!"

"I am in excruciating agony! Gangrene may be setting in!"

"Let's hope it's a colour she likes!"

At that moment Pip came sauntering back in, beaming at me. "Don't get up. Wanted to say thanks. Pat on the back."

Virginia wasn't to be placated. "It was a catastrophe."

"No. What you don't understand is that H.R.H. derives enormous plea-sure from making everyone around her as uncomfortable as possible. Today was a resounding success. We must do it again. She insists!"

"I'LL TUMBLE FOR YA'!"

RAYLEEN GIBSON
Professional Stuntwoman &
Chief Executive Officer of AAAH
(Aged Animal Actor's Home)

RAYLEEN GIBSON ON ROYALTY

What pisses me off about royalty is you have to learn all their names at school. It's so bloody confusing. You know, you've got William the First, followed by Henry the Second, then Charles the Third, and Malcolm the Fifth. I reckon they'd be easier to remember if they had names that showed their real character. Like George the Nutcase, Henry the Serial Killer, Edward the Shirt Lifter, Victoria the Fag Hag, right up to Charles the Jerk Who Ditched the Most Beautiful Woman in the World for a Woman Who Looks Like a Horse!

JANIE PILLSWORTH ON ROYALTY

Did you know that years ago President Tito asked Richard Burton and Elizabeth Taylor to become the king and queen of Yugoslavia? Isn't that an amazing idea? You know that today it would be like asking Demi Moore and Bruce Willis to become the king and queen of Estonia. Instead of Knights of the Round Table you would have the Knights of Planet Hollywood. Sir Sylvester Stallone and Lord Schwarzenegger. No doubt we would have to find a suitable country for Tom and Nicole to rule over. Hopefully their agents would advise them against it. Royalty is so ten minutes ago. ◆

BEAUX MIRAGE CONDOS
RETIREMENT COMMUNITY

FERN ROSENTHAL ON ROYALTY

I'll tell you who's royalty . . . Steve Lawrence and Eydie Gorme, that's who. They are the king and queen of good, clean music. Good clean music. And they've kept their looks so beautifully. Well, she's a little heavy, but he's a doll.

Ms. Hope Finch
P.O. Box 1749, Taconic Pkwy.
Connecticut
E-mail@www.lenslady.edu

*Helping to end animal
cruelty and abuse.*

Dear Harvey Weinstein,

    Let me introduce myself. My name is Hope
Finch, and I am a third-year film student at
Sweetbriar College, where I major in film studies at the Ida Lupino Department of Gynocentrism
and the Celluloid Image. I am sending my screenplay to you, Harvey, because you have shown your
dedication to the individual artiste's voice,

and also on the recommendation of my father, Douglas Finch, whom you met at the Fire and Ice Charity Ball, last December. He was sitting two tables across from you in the Patrons enclosure, with my godfather Orson Bean. I trust I have rung some bells?

The following screenplay is based on my own personal experience, and friends have likened it to a modern-day *Jules et Jim* (Jules and Jim). I would like to shoot it on 35mm black-and-white film, with an all-female crew, and although I'm open to suggestions, I think Lili Taylor is the only actress who can play "Me" with integrity and verisimilitude, and like me she unashamedly wears her underarm hair long. Prince "Al" should be played by the guy in the turban in another of your fine films, *The English Patient*. His name escapes me, but I'm sure your assistant can look it up.

Don't worry, you are the sole recipient of this original work. I will be at the Sundance Film Festival next week, staying at my Aunt Brooke's ski chalet, and can easily snowboard into town to meet you for lunch.

Looking forward to lensing with you,

Hope Finch

```
            THE PRINCE AND I
              by Hope Finch
```

WARNING!
This original work is copyrighted material and the
sole property of Finch Films and has been regis-
tered with the Library of Congress! Any usage or
reproduction thereof is prohibited by law and is
a punishable offense! (I know this sounds harsh,
but a friend of mine had a really bad experience
with an unscrupulous story editor on *Murphy Brown*
— 'nuff said.)

EXT. MARGARET SANGER HALL — LATE AFTERNOON

An establishing shot of a quasi-modern dorm amid
the trees and lawns and ponds of a pristine
eastern university campus. Push in to reveal the
sign above the door: "Margaret Sanger Hall."

                                        CUT TO:

INT. HALLWAY — SAME TIME

We see a series of doors with construction paper
cutouts in the shape of the female reproductive
system. Each ovary has a name on it. The camera
pans down the hall and stops at the door that
has the names HOPE DAVIS and CROSBY COLLINS in
ovaries.

                                        CUT TO:

INT. HOPE AND CROSBY'S DORM ROOM

HOPE DAVIS, a sweet-faced freshman wearing well-
worn Levi's and a soft sweatshirt, little makeup, and cool prescription glasses is sitting on
the floor in the center of the room carefully
painting a banner that reads, "WIMMIN'S COALI-
TION 'DATE A FEMINIST FOR FUNDS' AUCTION."

                    ME
          Crosby? Does this look even to you?
          I feel like I painted it slanty.

                  CROSBY
                (voice only)
            Oh, God! Yes! Yes!

WE PAN over to CROSBY's bed where we can't really see what she looks like, but we can certainly
tell that she is having intercourse with a
GENERIC NAKED COLLEGE GUY.   *Harvey, hope this does-*
                              n't make us NC-17, but
                    ME   *we need the reality here.*
          Crosby!! You're not even looking!

                                        CUT TO:

EXT. CAMPUS LAWN - DAY

A makeshift stage is set up with my banner
proudly flapping above it. Liz Phair's "FLOWER"
is playing from speakers on either side of the
stage, and a young "womyn," STEVIE, with a
severe haircut, nose ring, and a flannel shirt,
is standing behind a podium with a microphone.

                    STEVIE
        Our next sister available for an
        evening of companionable discourse
        and activity in exchange for funds
        with no implied oppression or
        obligation beyond what she herself
        deems appropriate is Hope Davis!

I strut up onto the stage and do a cuttingly
satirical rendition of a model's walk. I walk to
the microphone at center stage.

                    HOPE
        I love recycling, protest marches,
        and romantic dinners for two, but
        don't try to take me to McDonald's
        because I'm a vegetarian and Big Macs
        are ground from cattle grazed on
        deforested Brazilian land!

The audience cheers wildly. Stevie starts the
bidding.

                WOMAN NO. 1
        Twenty-five dollars!!

                    STEVIE
        That's twenty-five dollars. Are

there any more bids? Twenty-five
going once, twenty-five going twice . . .

                    PRINCE "AL"
          Five thousand dollars!!!

Everyone turns to see where this bid has come
from. We see Prince Al-Sayyid Hasanayn Ibn Hamid
Abdullah, or Prince "Al," a young Arab man in
Western clothing and sunglasses but wearing a
traditional headdress, has joined the crowd with
his bodyguards. Stevie points to him and shouts:

                    STEVIE
          Sold!

                                        CUT TO:

INT. PRIVATE ROOM AT AN ARAB RESTAURANT —
EVENING

Prince "Al," wearing a traditional robe, is
seated on cushions at the head of a long table
laden with platters of exotic foods. Several
bodyguards stand in corners of the room, Nusrat
Fateh Ali Khan plays from hidden speakers, and
at the other end of the table, under a black
abaya, sits a pair of dark eyes belonging to
Princess Nora. I enter nervously.

PRINCE "AL"
Come, sit next to me, radiant flower.

I notice Nora at the other end of the table
for the first time.

HOPE
Hi! I didn't even see you there! I'm
Hope. Don't we take "Peoples and
Plants" together?

PRINCE "AL"
Oh, that is just my wife, Princess
Nora. She is only taking one course
at the university.

NORA
I am taking women's Reebok step
class. I have greatly lowered my
resting heart rate. Sometimes I also
do abs, buns, and . . .

Prince "Al" interrupts.

PRINCE "AL"
That is enough talking, Nora.

HOPE
Hey, that's not very nice, Prince Al.

You're in America now, and here, we
have a little thing called free
speech. Now, what were you saying,
Nora?

                    NORA
               (nervously)
Um. Thighs. Abs, buns, and thighs.

               PRINCE "AL"
Hey! Hello! It's me, here. Prince
Al! I want some attention!

                    HOPE
Wow. That's really great that you
can be so in touch with your feelings
and just lay your neediness out there
like that!

               PRINCE "AL"
               (disarmed)
Um. Yes. I am a man of great
sensitivity. . . . Now, Nora! Serve us
some drink.

Nora gets up and begins filling glasses. The
servants begin filling large gold plates with
couscous and large hunks of animal flesh.

Note to Prop Master: This should be ↗
tofu, colored red with boiled beet juice.

                    HOPE
        Oh, G-d. I can't eat that. That's
        meat! I'm a total vegetarian except
        for sushi sometimes. Meat is murder.

Prince "Al" barks something in Arabic to the
servants, who pile rice up on my plate.

                    NORA
        I would like only rice, too, please.

Prince "Al" frowns at Nora. Her bravery dissi-
pates.

                    NORA
              (continuing; timidly)
        . . . and some lamb, please.

There is an awkward silence.

                 PRINCE "AL"
        This is big fun. Yes? We're going
        to party tonight!

                                      CUT TO:

MONTAGE—

We flash on scenes of the date in progress.

—Prince "Al" and I are disco dancing under flashing lights. Nora is dancing around. I pull her in to the dancing circle. Prince "Al" pushes her back out.

—Prince "Al" and Nora and I play Twister as one of the servants spins the spinner.

> SERVANT
> Your royal highness, left foot, green.

Closeup on the spinner going round and round — to show the passage of time.

CUT TO:

INT. DORM HALLWAY — LATE THAT NIGHT

Prince Al and I stand in front of my door.

> HOPE
> I really had a wonderful night, Prince Al. Thank you very much. And please thank Nora for me. Good night.

> PRINCE "AL"
> Good night? But the night has not been done yet! Hope . . . have you ever been with a Royal Prince before?

HOPE

Wow, you're really hung up on that
royal thing, huh? I like to think
that despite titles, people are
people.

PRINCE "AL"

Ah, Hope. You have no royalty in the
United States. You cannot understand
the exalted status of a prince.

HOPE

This is adapted from a free verse poem I performed at the "Allen Ginsberg" Coffee Collective © Finch Poems

Hey! We have royalty here in
America! We have the artist formerly
known as Prince. There's Earl Sheib,
who'll paint your car in under an
hour. We've got Traci Lords and
Jack Lord, and Lady and the Tramp,
Queen Latifah, Butterfly McQueen, and
Steve McQueen. And Kings. Where do
I start? Martin Luther King, Billie
Jean King, Nat King Cole, B.B. King,
Carole King, King Kong, and, of course,
the King himself — Elvis. John Wayne
was the duke and Babe Ruth was the
Sultan of Swat and Jim Morrison was
the Lizard King. We've got Sir Mix-a-lot,
Duke Ellington, Count Chockula,
Gladys Knight, Ted Knight, and, of

course, Chistopher Knight, who played
Peter on the original *Brady Bunch*.
You ever watch the *Brady Bunch*? I
used to have to beg my mother to let
me stay up and watch it . . .

                    PRINCE "AL"
You will be quiet now and come to my
room and we will make sex, yes?

                      HOPE
Gosh, Prince Al. You're really not
a very good listener, and despite
your honest, straightforward
verbalization of your desire to have
intercourse with me, you're married
and I don't think Nora . . .

                    PRINCE "AL"
But I have explained to Nora that I
have purchased you, and she
understands quite well!

                      HOPE
Whoa whoa whoa, wait. Back up here.
You helped fund the buses that the
"wimmin's" coalition chartered for
the pro-choice march on Washington,
and thanks to you we're getting the

air-conditioned ones with the
bathrooms and the reclining chairs,
but that was just for a date.

                    PRINCE "AL"
You mean, I did not purchase you for
my American sex slave? That was not
an American sex slave auction?

                    HOPE
Oh, gosh. Cross-cultural
communication can be so difficult
sometimes! I'm sorry, Prince "AL."
This was just a date for charity.

                    PRINCE "AL"
Oh, Hope. I am very disappointed.
I thought we were starting something
tonight. I even bought you a
convertible BMW and a beautiful
condominium off campus, where you
could live in splendor.

                    HOPE
You really did that?

                    PRINCE "AL"
Of course, with a hot tub and a Mr.
Steam.

                    HOPE
Oh, Prince "Al." I bet beneath that
misogynistic, macho bullshit, you're
a really great guy. But I want you
to go home to Nora and remind her
that you're still her Prince Charming.

                  PRINCE "AL"
How about you just show me your
breasts?   *He actually
                                    said this,
                    HOPE   yuck!!!*
Go home, "Al"!

                                        CUT TO:

INT. WIMMIN'S COALITION BUS TO WASHINGTON

Me and Nora are dressed in jeans and T-shirts
that say "Reproductive Freedom," sitting next to
each other on the bus and singing loudly with
the rest of the sisters, Helen Reddy's "I Am
Woman":

                HOPE/NORA/WIMMIN
    . . . if I have to, I can do anything!
I am strong! I am invincible! I am
WOMAN!

As the camera pulls back, in a helicopter shot above the bus, we see the following titles:

After the march on Wahington, Princess Nora changed her name to Kundalini, and with her lover, Debbie, formed a support group for other victims of female circumcision called "Mutilated but Not Mute."

Prince "Al" graduated from college with a master's degree in international finance and formed a corporation to develop a chain of theme parks called "Harem International." Before his dream was realized, he was struck down by bovine spongiform encephalopathy (Mad Cow Disease) from eating a beefburger prepared by his 27th wife.

Hope Finch went on to become an acclaimed filmmaker and won the Independent Spirit Award for her insightful movie on the tragic objectification of females in our culture, *The Jon Benet Ramsey Story*, starring Lourdes Leon.

Peace Y'all

THE END

CHAPTER
THREE
MOTHERS

TRACEY ULLMAN ON MOTHERS

Here is a picture of my mother when she was seventeen. It was 1946, and she'd just left home and joined the Land Army. She ploughed fields, milked cows, and drove trucks as Britain recovered from the war and manpower was low. I love this photograph of her, quite a "sweater girl" with a curious, expectant expression. My mum was very popular in the barracks because she played the piano and sang like Jeanette MacDonald.

My mother is now a pensioner who lives in Surrey, England; and although she no longer has room for a piano, she still makes an effort to sing like Jeanette MacDonald.

For my "Mothers" episode of *Tracey Takes On* I asked her to film an opening with me and she readily agreed, feeling it was about time that the general public be able to see where I get my talents from. We arrived with a film crew on a summer morning, and my mum busied herself brewing tea and opening cans of salmon for sandwiches. When we were ready to shoot, my husband, acting as director, told her to stand at her front door and hold her moving footstool of a dog, Sophie—who had eaten more sandwiches than any of us. That was the last command I remembered her obeying with any clarity. From that point on she turned to jelly. Her voice became unnaturally high, like John Cleese pretending to be a woman in a Monty Python sketch. "Hello darling!" she said, staring into the camera, sweat forming on her upper lip, eyes glazing. Sophie, sensing fear, started to wriggle violently, and Allan shouted "Cut!" but like a true amateur Mum continued, until she had been convinced that "the thing has been turned off, Doreen." After a lot of "Oh dear, it's not as easy as it looks"–type comments, we continued, and eventually we had enough footage to piece together. And anything she missed I figured I could dub later—if John Cleese wasn't available.

Mum's very proud of the finished piece, which also involves her grandchildren, whom she dotes on. I think it's invaluable to have us together on film; and my husband, ever the producer, is thrilled that for the first three minutes of the show he didn't have to pay any professional actors. She said the worst part about the day, was the stiff shoulder she had from holding Sophie up for minutes at a time. And like a typical mother she wrapped and froze the leftover sandwiches, saying we could eat them when we come to film the sequel.

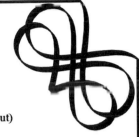

**Trevor Ayliss
& Barrington LeTissier
Willows Mews Cottage
Osterly on the Green
Middlesex, MD12 6HE**

(Come off the M40 at the Robin Hood Roundabout)

TREVOR AYLISS ON MOTHERS

My friend Keith's mother gave my adolescence its most shattering moment. She was a sexy thing, pencil skirt, mascara—even in the afternoon— and lashings of Je Reviens perfume by Worth. Every schoolboy's fantasy, except mine.

Anyhow, Keith had a birthday party and she got me coming out of the bathroom. I could smell the gin and tonic as she pressed her crimson lips on mine and grabbed me where no woman had grabbed me before, or since. I ran all the way home and was violently sick.

Me older brother found me and asked what happened. "It's that Keith's mother, isn't it?" he asked. I said yes. "Her what has the hair dressing salon in Corporation Street, with the tight skirts?" Right. "And it made you sick?" I nodded, yes it did. He looked at me for several moments, then he said: "I think we'd better get you to the doctor, our kid, you could be catching queer."

VAN NUYS SAVINGS & LOAN

KAY CLARK
ASSISTANT BRANCH MANAGER

KAY CLARK ON MOTHERS

I always wanted a pet, but with Mother allergic to everything, even her own skin, it's out of the question. But one day, as I was in the garden, Joey flew into my life. And left a little stain on my best cardigan.

Then the secrets and lies began. The strain of hiding a 7 oz. orange and grey cockatiel made me realise how that poor Frank family must have felt.

Joey learned to imitate me, and one day when I was out, he flew into Mother's room and kept saying, "Time for your medicine, dear. Time for your medicine, dear." Mother took sixteen doses of her diuretic before she realised it wasn't me, so Joey had to go. And so did Mother. She lost 22 pounds in nine minutes.

Now I keep no secrets from her except that I know when she's going to die—never! Mustn't say that. Naughty, naughty Kay, mustn't say that, mustn't, mustn't. . . .

A LARK WITH KAY CLARK

"HOW MANY PEOPLE DOES IT TAKE TO CHANGE A LIGHT BULB IN AN OFFICE?"

"WELL, JUST ONE... BUT IF IT WAS A SUCCESS, EVERYONE ELSE WOULD TAKE CREDIT FOR IT!"

RUBY ROMAINE ON MOTHERS

Personally, I think any more than two or three kids is not a family, it's a litter. Like these crazy Mexican ladies around here who keep poppin' out babies like they were gum balls. And then what happens? The little jumping beans run wild in the streets and they start to make more babies. Too much, if you ask me. I did things just right. I had Buddy and Desiree six months apart, and that way I could spend lots of time with them and make sure they were growing up right. I know Buddy might sometimes walk around the streets in my bathrobe screamin', "Stop the noise! Stop the noise!" And Desiree steals things from the morgue where she works, but they're good kids and I love

'em and neither one of them grew up to be a serial killer or one of these people who have sex with their pets, which is all you can hope for in this life, right? Hey, when I do a job, I do my best. The proof is in the pudding.

EARTH MOTHER TO ERIN.

By Jeremy Smith

THE OLD VINYL VIBES COLUMN

Today I met Erin McColl, former lead singer of Wisechild, *the* supergroup of the seventies. If you are one of the few people on the planet who haven't heard of the band, in your excuse you can always use the old adage of that bygone era, "If you remember it, you weren't really there." Wisechild were responsible for songs like "Momma Jinx," "Lost on a Highway," and, of course, "Sweet Lady Moonlight."

I arrive at the house in the Hollywood Hills and meet Erin outside on the deck. She sits in a hammock, wearing a blouse with a Mexican shawl round her shoulders. There's a guitar at her feet. It takes a few minutes before she notices me; it's a wind chime jangling in the breeze that shakes her out of her reverie.

"Yeah, I remember it like it was yesterday. I mean, it was my first album. Seminal, man. Probably the most important I ever made. Changed my life around. Before I was, like, working in this organic bookstore. Hangin' out at the Troubadour at night, hoping to meet Steven Stills. . . . We cut the tracks in this funky little studio in Malibu, off PCH. . . ."

At this point a woman appears with some tea, "No, Erin, it was in Hollywood." This is Dusty Roads, Erin's manager, who's been with her through everything. She puts down the tea.

"Hollywood?" Erin says, a little confused.

"Was yours the chamomile or papaya leaf?"

"Chamomile—wait you could be right. Sunset Sound! That's where I put down

Feedback Magazine, July 10–24, 1997

'Sweet Lady Moonlight.'" She picks up her guitar and starts to sing,

> *Another sunrise on Mulholland,*
> *With the smog beneath her feet.*
> *I go running down the canyon. . . .*

She trails off, unable to remember the next line. "I think I wrote that one on mushrooms that some guy brought in from Taos. I think the Eagles were backing me."

Dusty shakes her head at me, no.

"And I think Dennis Hopper dropped by one night and broke all the windows." Erin breaks into another song,

> *Blue Jay mor—or—ning*
> *Whispers of sunlight*
> *Last night's wine still crimson in*
> *   the glass. . .*

"Joni gave me that line. 'Crimson in the glass,' I mean. Jesus, she could've used that herself, y'know? We met in France."

Dusty interrupts again, "We were in Bali, Erin."

"Bali? Oh man, yeah. It was so beautiful, we went to this harmonic convergence, and we slept on the beach and bought these beautiful scarves and put up a parking lot."

"It wasn't a parking lot, honey, we helped build a bamboo schoolhouse."

"Whatever. The album went platinum." Erin waits to be corrected before she continues, but Dusty nods—apparently she's right. "My business manager put the money in the Cayman Islands. You could only get to the bank at low tide. Then he died in a snorkeling accident."

"They never found the body."

"They never found my fuckin' money. . . ."

"That's why we put out the live album," Dusty says, turning to me. Suddenly a guitar pick hits her in the eye, "What's with this 'we' shit?!" Erin is energized for the first time, "Like, you wrote the songs? Like, you made my records? When I played Monterey was that you on stage next to me or someone called Janis?!" There's a brief pause.

"You never played Monterey. When Janis Joplin died you were still at school."

"That's right!" Erin is righteous now, "You don't forget shit like that." She starts singing again,

> *Barefoot on Topanga*
> *Chasing down the lines*
> *I can hear the reasons*
> *Jus' can't make the rhymes. . . .*

The song trails off and Erin lies back in the hammock. Seemingly exhausted, she promptly falls asleep. Dusty covers her with a blanket and then shows me out, making sure that I have tickets for Erin's appearance at the Van Nuys Pro-Choice rally on Sunday. "She's still the greatest. Come backstage, we'll have some Snapple with Tiny Tim's widow and Melanie," says the manager/agent/publicist/nursemaid and earth mother to Erin. Come in, Erin. ■

Feedback Magazine, July 10–24, 1997

MANHATTAN REVIEW MAGAZINE

from the editor's desk.

FACSIMILE COVER SHEET

To: Dr. Stuart Trabulus
Company: Park Avenue Psychiatric Associates
Phone: (212) 264-4177
Fax: (212) 264-4183

From: Janie Pillsworth
Company: Manhattan Review Magazine
Phone: (212) 650-6997
Fax: (212) 650-5054

Date: 5/17/97

Pages: 3 (including cover page)

S—

Terribly sorry, Stuart, but I'm going to have to miss our session again today. I'm up to my supersternal notch in our September Preview issue, and I simply can't get away. However, I had a perfectly dreadful experience last evening that I felt certain you'd want to know about. I thought it best to get it all down for you before I forget any of the hideous details.

I was home, getting a massage after a particularly brutal day, when I smelt the cloying, sickly sweet odor of chocolate chip cookies baking in the kitchen. Twan had to light another aromatherapy candle! Post-shiatsu, I investigated and found my mother and Olivia baking away—supposedly for a school picnic at Dalton. I told my mother not to bother, that I'd order Norri rolls from Zen Palate. I generously let pass the *appalling* banality of the cookie idea (I had visions of her sending the children to school clutching round cookie tins with Currier & Ives Christmas motifs! Can you imagine?), but Mother, completely unprovoked, began needling me about going to the school picnic, even though she *knew* I had the Rifat Ozbek Preview the same day. Then, to my horror, *she* volunteered to go herself. I could barely open my mouth to object before she accused me of being embarrassed about her in front of my friends and associates. Well, rather than deny it, I spoke from my heart, Stuart, because I've learned from you to honor my feelings. I mean, honestly, she would be completely out of place among my friends—she'd probably talk about knitting patterns, or "The War" and how she survived on drippings and powdered egg! She claimed she'd "like to get out a bit more, that's all," as if I were holding her prisoner in the apartment and forcing her at gunpoint to crochet those hideous antimacassars of hers!

As you might imagine, I was rigid with tension at this point, my shiatsu a mere memory. I tried to explain, as patiently as I could, how unreasonable she was being. But she just doesn't get it, Stuart! I mean, after Daddy died, I opened my doors to her. If she didn't have Olivia and Daniel to look after, she'd be moping around some horribly depressing flat with nothing to do. She has her own VCR, which I bought her, she sleeps on last season's Pratesi linens, and she has a fabulous address!

As if all this weren't enough to push me over the edge, Olivia came into the kitchen at that point and accused me of being "nasty" to her "Granny!" The fact that Olivia would make such a rude remark to me is only further proof that Mother is entirely too lax with the children. But I held my tongue and only asked that Olivia please try to remember to refer to Mother as "Grandmother" or "Nanny." Then, Olivia turned to me and said the most cutting, unkind thing of all. She said, "You'll be old one day. You should remember that."

Well, I'd had enough *sturm und drang* for one evening. I decided to take a Xanax, put on my Concorde eyeshades, and go straight to bed. I *thought* I'd put the whole event out of my mind, but I was awakened hours later by the most ghastly, harrowing nightmare! It started off pleasantly enough—I was an elegant older woman going to the opening of my daughter's chic little gallery down in Soho. As I tried to enter, I was rudely stopped by two skanky, *downtown*-sort-of-girls at the door. Not only did they claim not to know who I was, but they kept referring to me in the most offhand way as "Mrs. Billsworth!" I became infuriated and pushed past the grubby twosome. And there they were—Olivia and Daniel (!) all grown up, looking fabulous. I demanded to know why my name wasn't on the list. Daniel mumbled something unintelligible and deferred to Olivia, who gave me some pathetic excuse about it not being my "scene," but it was all too clear from their exasperated expressions that they didn't want me there. I thought I'd remind them just exactly who I'd been: the High Priestess of Hip, the Icon of Trend, dear friend of Brad and Gwyneth, Warren and Annette, Johnny and Kate—it was I who had snubbed Bruce and Demi before anyone else—I'd sailed with the Perlmans and skied with the Spielbergs, Helmut Newton once photographed me wearing something rubber on a llama, Princess Diana had me on her fucking speed dial!! I felt sure that would put them in their place, but they just looked at me coolly and said, "I'm sorry—who are you?" Then Daniel set two security guards on me, and I woke up screaming.

I was in quite a state—convinced my children hated me, but Mother was there at my bedside, comforting me. We actually shared a nice little moment. You're always telling me I should experiment with being vulnerable—and I think I might have been, for a few seconds. But then Mother tried making me tea with *tap* water, and the moment was spoiled.

Then, Stuart, this morning, as I was getting out of my town car on Madison, I thought I saw the grown-up Olivia and Daniel come out of Prada and duck into an alley to avoid me. Does this qualify as a hallucination of some sort, and if so, could it be caused by mixing my Zoloft with Ativan, Chardonnay, and Phen-fen?

Which reminds me. I know you're the best in the business with a pad, Stuart, but I'm just not happy with the Zoloft. My orgasms still aren't up to par, even with the vibrator and the other thing. A friend of mine went off Prozac and started Paxil, and she's having fabulous orgasms again. Write me up a slip for sixty and I'll have my assistant swing by and pick it up this afternoon. Better yet, do you have any free samples?

Fax me your thoughts on the dream, etc., although I've got Bruce Weber cooling his heels outside my office and Joan Didion after, so who knows when I'll get a chance to read it. I do feel loads better though. You're a genius.

love,

J.

La Granger

9820 Valley Star Dr.
Sherman Oaks, CA 91423

FAX COVER SHEET

To: Marmalade Granger

♥ Linda Granger

My Darling Marmalade:

I'm so sorry for my burst of emotion over the news that I am about to become a —I still find it difficult to write/say/or type it —gtsndnithed ggendother grandmother (my nails were skittering all over the keyboard as I tapped that out). But after a long talk to my inner self in my vanity mirror, I emerged consoled and shouted from my poolside lanai, "My baby is having a baby!"

I wasn't going to say anything, darling, but I did notice you were carrying a little extra weight, and I was praying silently to my higher power that you weren't perpetuating the eating disorders that have plagued my life. But no.

page 1 of 9 received

It seems like only yesterday when I saw you in your bassinet, kicking your little legs; and I called you Marmalade because that's what the lawyers served on muffins when I signed the adoption papers.

I may not have been a perfect mommy. I know it was hard for you when I was an active alcoholic and bulimic and going through my battles with cancer and Dexatrim, but I always tried. I got you that talcum powder commercial that's still paying royalties, I never spoke to Jimmy Caan again after he made that pass at you at the beach house, you had the best seats at tapings, and I always found you a new daddy whenever you needed one.

Now there's so much to do, so much to plan. The baby shower on *Access Hollywood*, the delivery room photo rights for *People* magazine, my entry in the Most Glamorous Grandmother in America Competition. And just think of all the invitations to Disney movie premieres!

Oh, Marmie, this couldn't have come along at a better time in my career, look what it's done for Jane Seymour. . . .

`page 2 of 9 received . . . fax out of paper`

H.R.H. ON MOTHERS

PIP

Mother Teresa, Your Highness.

H.R.H.

Oh. I was in India once as a girl. We stayed with the Maharajah of Vindaloo, or was it Madras? I never remember. All those places sound like curries. I remember the day that our dear Ayah, that's Indian for Nanny, took us for an awfully uncomfortable walk in the palace grounds to admire the local flora and fauna . . . and she got eaten by a tiger. We laughed for days.

I expect you want a donation. Perhaps a new tea towel for your head. We still have some with "I survived the Windsor Castle Fire" written on them. Talk to Pip. Good-bye.

FERN ROSENTHAL ON MOTHERS

The following phone conversation was recorded on Felice Valks' answering machine, the night that Fern and Harry welcomed their grandson Ryan into the world.

Felice: Hello, we're asleep.
    . . .
Fern: Felice? Is that you? You sound terrible, you gotta switch to menthol!
    [Answerphone picks up.]
    Hello, Felice and George are away from the phone right now . . .

Fern: Now you sound better!
    [Message continues] *. . . but please talk to us . . . .*
Felice: I don't know how to turn the machine off, Fern. . . .
Fern: What?
    [Message] *Leave your message after Mr. Sinatra stops singing "New York, New York!"*
Fern: Oy, my favorite!
Felice: Saul, clap on the lights, it's Fern.
    [Message]—*Neeuw YooorrrrK! . . . BEEEP.*
Felice: Finally! Now Fern, why are you calling me at this time of night, has Harry had another heart attack?!

Fern: Oh please, Felice. The baby's here!

Felice: Mazeltov!

Fern: Yes, we have a grandson! I'm calling you from Sheila's bedroom. He has such a gorgeous nose, just like my family. You wouldn't know he was Jewish. Oh my God! Hold on Felice. . . . Harry, put out that cigar. You're gonna give the kid a tumor!!

　　[Slapping sound]

Felice: So Fern, you're in Sheila's bedroom? She's home from the hospital already?

Fern: What hospital? This crazy daughter of ours has just squeezed a matzoh ball through a straw—without drugs—on an Ikea futon!

Felice: Where does she think she's living, Minsky Pinsk?

Fern: She didn't even have a doctor, Felice!

Felice: Don't tell me *you* delivered the baby.

Fern: Are you kidding, she threw an ice cube at me and told me to F— U—C—K off! No, there's some midwife called Gwen with crystals and meshugge whales singing! And if she makes one more comment about my negative energy, I'm gonna smack the shiksa-hairy-legged bitch into next Tuesday! I just hope she washed her hands.

Felice: Lysol everything!

Fern: I did. I wasn't taking any chances, Felice. We had an ambulance right outside, and Doctor Weinberg was on a beeper minutes away.

Felice: You're so smart. Saul, I'm awake now, make some Swiss Miss.

　　[Male voice in background]

Felice: What's Grandpa saying, Fern?

Fern: He's telling me to relax, he says in some countries pregnant women squat in the field, out comes a baby, plop, in the soil. The mother sticks it on her nipple and keeps plowing. Harry, please . . . and in some countries people wipe their ass with their hands. This is America. And do you think those field babies grow up to be certified public accountants?

Felice: Spoken like a true grandmother. Ah Fernola, remember the night your Sheila was born?

Fern: Of course I remember.

Felice: Harry and Saul were out in the lobby eating smoked fish and bagels.

Fern: Yeah, and I was in a room with you, numb from the waist down.

Felice: I was numb from the waist down? Who told you that? Did Saul say I'm numb from the waist down?

Fern: No Felice, *I* was numb from the waist down.

Felice: Oh, I thought you were saying that I . . .

Fern: Shut up, darling. Anyway, Sheila popped out, I waved hello, she gave a squawk, they put her in my arms, you took a Polaroid, and Harry came in and gave me big jewelry, remember? Now that's the way to have a baby . . . high as a kite in a good clean hospital!

Felice: The young husbands today, they want to be involved. They worry they're gonna miss something.

Fern: They miss nothing. Men should go away, not stand between a wife's legs with a video camera. One look at that big head coming out of there, and a man's going to be shtupping his secretary before you can say episiotomy!

Felice: Oh. Does your son-in-law have a secretary, Fern?

Fern: All I know is that the putz is out in the garden now, burying the placenta.

Felice: You're kidding. If we did that our Pomeranian Ginger would dig it right up. Now Fern, did you tell Sheila about Dr. Gitlin? He's the top varicose vein man in the tristate area.

Fern: I'll tell her . . . Sheila, Sheila! Oh my God, Felice, she's trying to breast-feed! Sheila, don't get involved with that. It takes all the starch out of them!

Felice: Fern, calm down, take a Xanax, go be with your grandchild. Your baby had a baby. It's the miracle of life.

Fern: You're right. You're so wise, darling. I'll see you at the bris.

Felice: All right, dollface.

    [Female voice in background]

    [Female scream]

    [Telephone receiver dropped]

Felice: Fern, what's happening?

Fern: Sheila just said she's not having the baby circumcised!

Felice: Aaah! I just spit the Swiss Miss all over my comforter!

Fern: Okay, fine Sheila. Break my heart. You be the one every day with the damn Q-tip! You be the one who has to explain to him why he's different when he's showing his schmeckle to the other boys behind the Temple!

Felice: If he has it done when he's older, tell her, it's considered major surgery. People have bled to death!

    [Telephone receiver dropped]

    [Male voice]

Harry: Felice, it's Harry. We gotta hang up now. We've got twenty-two more calls to make, just on Fern's side of the family.

Felice: I understand, darling, where's Fern?

Harry: She ran out to the drugstore in her bare feet, to get Similac. [shouting] FERN, BE CAREFUL OF THAT HOLE IN THE YARD! Oy, Christ, Felice, she's covered in placenta, I gotta go get paper towels.

Line goes dead. Machine switches off. The event has been recorded for posterity.

The Tara Estates

"A Gated & Graceful Community"

Birdie Godsen

BIRDIE GODSEN ON MOTHERS

My son, Bob Junior, has a birthday tomorrow. He turns eight, which of course means it's time for him to get his first gun. My husband Robert bought him a very nice twelve gauge, but then my father showed up this afternoon with the most gorgeous rifle I've ever seen — a semiautomatic with a scope and everything. Somebody was going to have hurt feelings. I put my arms around both of them and said, "My son is so blessed — his father and his granddaddy both love him so much he's getting *two* firearms for his birthday!"

Disaster averted! Now, the only problem is: what's his ever-loving mother gonna get him? His little sister already got him this variety pack of ammo — birdshot, buckshot, hollowpoint, and dumdums. He's been begging me for a minibike, but I just don't know. He's only eight, and I hear those things can be very dangerous. But then, I'm a mother, and I guess it's my job to worry.

THE
GYPSY
CAB
COMPANY

CHIC ON MOTHERS

Since me and my brother move here twenty years ago, we been trying to save up enough money to bring my dear mother over from the Old Country. First time we have the money saved, I have to use it as a bribe to get my hack license. We save enough money again, but then my brother has to have emergency surgery — he has to have hair transplant. I was the donor; they took it off the back of my hands . . . I don't even miss it. Finally, last week we have enough money again. But at last minute, we decide to take a coupla chicks to see Victor/Victoria. So, tomorrow, like the good sons that we are, we start saving all over again.

CHAPTER
FOUR
CRIME

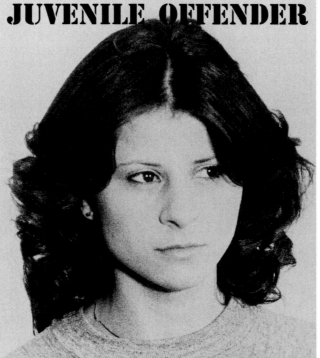

BRITISH TRANSPORT POLICE

JUVENILE OFFENDER

#A453-74800DG

TRACEY ULLMAN ON CRIME

I got into trouble with the law once in my life. I was thirteen years old, and I used to travel every day to my performing arts school by train. This was a long, boring journey, but it became a lot of fun when another pupil, Richard King, joined me en route. Being young performers just bursting to share our talents, we started entertaining the other passengers on the 07:37 to Waterloo. We would tap dance down the aisles singing "Good morning" and chucking the chins of shy British commuters. If this failed to get their attention, we would lie in the luggage racks like Eartha Kitt, or pretend to get sucked out the window.

We thought we were just great, and so did a few of the passengers, and we built up a following of mousy secretaries and civil servants who felt that we brightened up their dull lives. This boosted our confidence no end, and we were constantly trying to think up new entertainments. Richard was living away from his home in the North and boarded with a woman who was an awful cook. So he would bring the previous night's dinner with him in a plastic bag, and when we were at speed, he would hurl it out the window. And our audience got to see lamb stew, carrots, and cabbage smash against a tunnel wall. Unfortunately, we didn't stop at lamb stew, and when we smashed an apple cider bottle going over Twickenham bridge, an irate bespectacled man threw down his copy of *The Times* and pulled the emergency cord.

We were booked by the British Transport Police and put on probation for a couple of months. This entailed having a large woman with a mustache visit us in the principal's office at our school, and ask if we'd had any violent urges that month. It served its purpose: It scared the life out of me!

We were quiet on the train now, I buried my nose in my homework and read George Orwell's *1984*. Our mousy fans would look longingly at us, hoping for a burst of ABBA, or a panty-revealing high kick, but we were marked criminals now, and daren't run the risk.

MRS. NOH NANG NING ON CRIME

I HAD LEGAL PROBLEM 'CAUSE OF DONUT . . . BAD DONUT. SUPPOSED TO HAVE VANILLA ON TOP BUT INSTEAD HAD FINGER. FINGER FROM STUPID NEPHEW WHO WORK IN KITCHEN AND WHACK OFF HIS OWN FINGER WITH BIG KNIFE. STUPID BOY . . . LIKE HIS MOTHER WHO SLEPT WITH SOLDIERS. FINGER FELL IN FROSTING . . . FROSTING GO ON DONUT. MAN ASK FOR VANILLA DONUT, BUT HE GET <u>FINGER</u> DONUT. OH, MY GOD . . . SCREAMING, THIS MAN. SAY HE GONNA HIRE LAWYER, BUT HE ATE EVIDENCE. NO CASE. MY STUPID NEPHEW SORRY, TOO. STUPID BOY GOT NINE FINGER NOW. I SEND HIM BACK HOME. LOT OF PEOPLE WITH NINE FINGER THERE. LOT OF PEOPLE WITH NO FINGER THERE! IN MY COUNTRY NO UNSOLVED CRIMES. THEY CUT OFF YOUR HAND — AND THEN HOPE THAT YOU DID IT.

RUBY ROMAINE ON CRIME

I got arrested once. I was innocent, of course. It was one of those low-budget shows. It was all about people turning into rats. I was doing body makeup, and my job was to blend the skin where the tails attached to the extras' behinds. Believe me, it was unpleasant work. The thing is, there were a lot of people on this show sniffing up that cocaine crap. I never cared for it myself. But, years ago, I did let a gaffer rub some on my nipple and lick it off. He got a bigger kick out of it than I did, that's for sure. Any-hoo, the police came and searched the whole set. Guess where they found a half a pound of pure Colombian nose candy? In the hair and makeup trailer. They took us all downtown. One of the girls was black and of course she was found guilty. But, you know, what is a crime? That movie went straight to video, and it was some of my best work. You rent it, freeze the frame, and I challenge you to spot where the rats' tails end and the actors' butts begin.

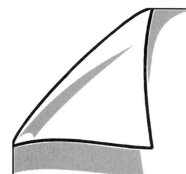

<u>Wimpman, KROSS, and Wussman</u>
"You name it, we'll sue it." *(Since 1987)*
PENTHOUSE
F. LEE BAILEY LEGAL CENTER
100 CANON DRIVE
BEVERLY HILLS

SYDNEY KROSS ON CRIME

This is the court transcript from my favorite case.

Enjoy!

SUPERIOR COURT OF THE STATE OF CALIFORNIA

COUNTY OF LOS ANGELES
PRESIDING: HON. HARRIET MASSINGBERD

GENEVIEVE LA DONVILLE   MICHAEL MORRIS DAVEEN

(Self-employed, Exotic Dancer)   VS.   (CEO of Speznik Products)

(PLAINTIFF)   (DEFENDANT)

COURT REPORTER'S TRANSCRIPT OF PROCEEDINGS

AUGUST 10, 1996
* * *

THE COURT: COUNSEL FOR THE PLAINTIFF MAY PROCEED.

MS. KROSS: LADIES AND GENTLEMEN OF THE JURY. MY CLIENT, GENEVIEVE LA DONVILLE, IS AN EXOTIC DANCER. LAST JANUARY FIFTEENTH, WHILE WAITING TO PERFORM AT THE CRYSTAL HOT STRIP-A-GO-GO EMPORIUM, SHE INADVERTENTLY SAT ON A SOUP-IN-A-POT CONTAINER, CONTAINING HOT CREAM OF MUSHROOM SOUP. THE SERIOUS SCALDING THAT SHE RECEIVED RESULTED IN A CIRCULAR SCAR ON HER RIGHT BUTTOCK. MAY IT PLEASE THE COURT TO SEE THE EVIDENCE?

THE COURT: PROCEED.

THE PLAINTIFF STANDS UP AND WALKS OVER TO THE JURY.

MS. KROSS: FURTHERMORE, SHE IS CONTINUALLY BEING HUMILIATED, AS CUSTOMERS HAVE TAKEN TO CALLING OUT, "BRING ON THE GIRL WITH THE CIRCLE ON HER ASS." OKAY, GENEVIEVE.

THE PLAINTIFF TURNS HER BACK ON THE JURY AND RAISES HER SKIRT.

[*See enclosed court artist's sketch*]

THE COURT: THAT'LL BE ENOUGH, THANK YOU, MISS LA DONVILLE.

PLAINTIFF: SURE.

THE PLAINTIFF RETURNS TO HER SEAT.

MS. KROSS: THE PROSECUTION CALLS MR. MICHAEL MORRIS DAVEEN TO THE STAND.

DIRECT EXAMINATION

BY MS. KROSS:

Q. MR. DAVEEN. SOON AFTER YOU BECAME MANAGING DIRECTOR OF SPEZNIK HOT DRINKS VENDING MACHINES, YOU ORDERED THE VENDING TEMPERATURE OF THE DRINKS TO BE INCREASED FROM 150 DEGREES TO 200, CORRECT?

A. YES.

Q. WHY DID YOU DO THAT?

A. BECAUSE RESEARCH HAD SHOWN THAT PEOPLE PREFER THE DRINKS TO BE HOTTER.

Q. TWO HUNDRED DEGREES IS VERY HOT, IS IT NOT?

A. IT'S PRETTY HOT, YES.

Q. SO, IF SOMEONE WERE TO SIT ON SOUP AT THAT TEMPERATURE, YOU WOULD EXPECT THEM TO BE SCALDED?

A. WE DIDN'T DESIGN THE PRODUCT TO BE SAT ON. PEOPLE NORMALLY DRINK IT.

THE DEFENDANT SMILES, THERE IS LAUGHTER IN THE COURTROOM.

Q. WHAT TEMPERATURE IS THE AIR YOU ARE SITTING ON, MR. DAVEEN?

A. I'M SORRY?

Q. ARE YOU WEARING BOXER SHORTS, MR. DAVEEN?

A. NO.

Q. YOU'RE WEARING THE OTHER KIND?

A. YES.

Q. REGULAR, CHEAP UNDERPANTS.

A. YES. [*RESENTFULLY*]

Q. AND THE TEMPERATURE OF THE AIR THAT IS TRAPPED BETWEEN YOUR BUTTOCKS AND YOUR UNDERPANTS, WHAT TEMPERATURE WOULD YOU SAY THAT AIR WAS?

A. IT VARIES.

LAUGHTER IN THE COURTROOM.

Q. OH, I GET IT. A FART JOKE. MR. DAVEEN, WHEN YOU WERE AT COLLEGE, DO YOU RECALL A VENDING MACHINE IN THE CAFETERIA?

A. UH, I THINK THERE WAS ONE, YES.

Q. AND WAS THERE ANYTHING SPECIAL ABOUT THIS MACHINE?

A. WELL, IF YOU PUT THE MONEY IN AND PUSHED COFFEE WITH NO SUGAR, IT GAVE YOU HOT CHOCOLATE.

Q. THAT'S RIGHT, AND WAS THERE ANYTHING ELSE WRONG WITH IT?

A. [*BECOMING AGITATED AT THE MEMORY*] WELL, IT WAS ALL WRONG. YOU PUSHED TEA, AND IT GAVE YOU SOUP. YOU PUSHED SOUP, IT GAVE YOU BLACK COFFEE. IT NEVER SAID WHAT IT WAS GOING TO GIVE YOU.

Q. SO, IT MADE YOU FEEL ANGRY?

A. YES!

Q. BECAUSE IT HAD TAKEN AWAY YOUR CONTROL, IT HAD TAKEN AWAY YOUR RIGHT TO CHOOSE?

A. [*WARMING TO THE IDEA*] YES!

Q. SO YOU KICKED IT, DIDN'T YOU? YOU KICKED IT, AND PUNCHED IT, AND CALLED IT NAMES?

A. YES. IT WAS A STUPID MACHINE!

Q. BECAUSE THAT MACHINE WAS TREATING YOU LIKE A CHILD. IT WAS TELLING YOU WHAT TO DO, IT WAS SAYING, YOU, A GROWN ADULT, ARE NOT RESPONSIBLE ENOUGH TO DECIDE WHAT YOU WANT. YOU WANTED COFFEE. IT SAID: "NO, MICHAEL, YOU CANNOT HAVE COFFEE, YOU WILL HAVE SOUP."

A. WHY DID IT DO THAT?

Q. THAT MACHINE WAS YOUR PARENT. A BIG STEEL PARENT WITH BLINKING LIGHTS AND NO SMILE, AND NO HUGS, AND NO BEDTIME STORY, AND NO DABBING ANTISEPTIC ON YOUR KNEE WHEN YOU FELL OFF YOUR SKATEBOARD, CORRECT?

A. [*QUIETLY*] YES.

Q. AND WHEN YOU KICKED IT, AND SHOUTED AT IT, YOU WERE TRYING TO HURT IT. YOU WERE TRYING TO HURT YOUR PARENTS!

A. YES.

Q. AND SO YOU GREW UP, YOU BECAME SUCCESSFUL, YOU BOUGHT THE VENDING COMPANY, AND SAW THE CHANCE TO HURT THAT BIG PARENT EVEN MORE BY INCREASING THE TEMPERATURE OF THE LIQUID INSIDE,

SO IT WOULD BURN THE MACHINE AND CAUSE IT AS MUCH PAIN AS IT CAUSED YOU! AS YOUR PARENTS CAUSED YOU! THOSE SAME HEARTLESS PARENTS WITH THE BLINKING GREEN LIGHTS IN THEIR EYES WHO NEVER LISTENED TO YOU, WHO GAVE YOU SOUP IN- STEAD OF COFFEE, WHO NEVER LET YOU BE YOU, WHO NEVER LOVED YOU! IS THAT RIGHT, MR. DAVEEN?!!?

A. YES. [*BREAKING DOWN*]

Q. [*SOFTLY*] AND IN YOUR OBSESSIVE QUEST FOR RE- VENGE, YOU HAVE LEFT THE INDELIBLE MARK OF RET- RIBUTION ON THE SOFT, INNOCENT SKIN OF GENEVIEVE LA DONVILLE.

MR. DAVEEN IS CRYING, THE PLAINTIFF IS CRYING, SO IS THE ENTIRE JURY. EVEN JUDGE MASSINGBERD IS DABBING AT HER EYES.

MS. KROSS: NO FURTHER QUESTIONS, YOUR HONOR.

MS. KROSS WALKS BACK TO THE PLAINTIFF AT HER DESK. JUROR NO. 8 (AN OLDER GENTLEMAN) RAISES HIS HAND.

OLD JUROR: EXCUSE ME, DO YOU THINK WE COULD SEE THE EVIDENCE ONE MORE TIME?

"I'LL TUMBLE FOR YA!"

RAYLEEN GIBSON
Professional Stuntwoman &
Chief Executive Officer of AAAH
(Aged Animal Actor's Home)

RAYLEEN GIBSON ON CRIME

I'd like to say, I think you have too many laws in the U.S. of A. And some of 'em are mean and unfair. Like, some idiot passed a law against dwarf tossing. What's that all about, I'd like to know? I used to be the number-one woman dwarf hurler in the state, and I won some nice prizes—a salad spinner, CD player, socket wrench set. Not to mention that's how I met my husband, Mitch. I stepped up to the tossing line one fine night, and somebody handed him to me. I looked down into his little eyes, a thrill went through me, and I almost didn't want to throw him. I won an AM/FM clock radio that night and the man of my dreams. Shouldn't be a law against that!

BEAUX MIRAGE CONDOS
RETIREMENT COMMUNITY

FERN ROSENTHAL ON CRIME

Whenever Harry and I hear that a crime has been committed, the first thing that comes to mind is, "Is this gonna hurt the Jews?" Going way back, I remember the day that Jack Ruby killed that Oswald maniac. We couldn't believe that Jack Ruby was Jewish. The next Friday night at Synagogue, I was, by the way, wearing a white suede top. I'll never do that again. What was I talking about? . . . Oh yeah, the Rabbi. My short-term memory is nonexistent since they put me on hormones. When the Jews all over the world found out that Son of Sam was David Berkowitz, there were "geshries" from here to tomorrow. They didn't calm down until they found out, thank God, he was adopted. And then, horror of horrors, Robert Shapiro had to be the first lawyer on O.J.'s team? That wasn't good for the Jews. Where does a Jewish boy come to represent someone who played football, a game that Jewish mothers have protected their sons from for decades? I want to believe that he didn't get into a good law school.

Bugge Manor (Since 1578)

Virginia Bugge
& Timothy Bugge
(M.P. for Greater Diddlesbury)
Bugge Manor
Wrencham Hollow
Diddlesbury

VIRGINIA BUGGE ON CRIME

It doesn't seem terribly long ago when there was a policeman on every corner who would tip his helmet and say, "Good evening, Ma'am," and one would say, "Good evening, Constable," back, and feel quite reassured that he was truly there to protect and serve.

And if one's brother had stolen apples, or put LSD in the water supply, the policeman would come 'round to the house and have a cup of tea and say, "There'll be no more of those high jinx, will there, Master Bugge?"

A few weeks ago, I was at a cocktail party in London in my husband Timmy's absence. And an old friend, Hugh Latimer, asked me to drive him back to his flat. I knew Hugh vaguely from our days in the Young Conservatives. Very attractive man and, rumor has it, terribly well endowed. Apparently, when he was at Eton, he was excused shorts in gym.

Anyway, when we pulled up at his flat, a police car was right behind us. "Better come in, old thing," said Hugh, "or the Boys in Blue will have you for driving under the influence." So we went in, waited in the hall, and the police just sat there. So Hugh persuaded me to go upstairs.

An hour later, they were still there. Hugh suggested I have a coffee and slipped off my coat. "They'll only collar you if you go down there," he warned me. "Walk a straight line, recite the alphabet backwards, and take a urine sample." Ghastly thought.

So it did make enormous sense to stay put, and Hughie—I was calling him Hughie by then—opened a second bottle of Dom and put on a CD of Tubular Bells. . . .

I'm not quite sure when the police gave up and left, but I do think Hughie's gym master had a point.

BIRDIE GODSEN ON CRIME

Through my church, I've gotten involved in volunteering at the state prison, so I see the result of crime close up. I counsel death row inmates. Not like that nun you hear so much about. I counsel them to accept that the death penalty is fitting and just, and then to get it over with quickly so as to save everybody a lot of heartache and time and money. It's very satisfying work. Sometimes I think I get more out of it than they do!

820 Valley Star Dr. Sherman Oaks, CA 91423

Dear Parole Board,

I'm writing in regard to Douglas Lund (you may know him better as Prisoner #66678722), who accosted me last year in a terrifying drama that began with him stalking me through Victoria's Secret (Sherman Oaks), followed by a death-defying car chase that led us to a deserted earthquake-damaged building. He hunted me through the hallways, engaging me in a deadly game of cat and mouse that culminated in a climactic scene where I was left hanging from a sixth-floor balcony (thank God for extra-strength acrylic nails and the police SWAT team). If you missed it on the network news, it is still available on videotape from CNN under the title "Granger in Danger."

Recently I received a letter from Douglas on the anniversary of his stalking me, saying that he was up for parole and asking if I might put in a good word on his behalf. He wrote that through therapy he realized that he'd fantasized a relationship between us and was now completely over his "Linda Granger Obsession." As someone who's not only played a psychologist on television but also been in therapy ever since it became popular, I know when somebody is just repeating what their doctor wants to hear. Been there, done that!

I couldn't help but wonder why things had cooled off so quickly between us, so I decided to drop by San Quentin to speak with Douglas in person. When I arrived, one of your charming guards, Santos, valet-parked my Cadillac and ushered me in through the VIP entrance. I was fascinated by this world of incarceration and just stood there inhaling the pungent scent of raw man and carbolic soap. I stored it in my memory as subtext to use in an upcoming audition for a new series called *She's the Warden*. Wish me luck!

When I was finally brought to the visiting area, I noticed that Douglas was paler, a bit thinner, and that his hand shook slightly as he chained-smoked his cigarettes. But he still had the same tempestuous fire in his eyes that had led him to threaten my life at knifepoint.

We chitchatted about old times for a while, and then out of the blue he asked me if I knew Tori Spelling (I haven't met her but I do know her father Aaron—I once went to an ice hockey game in his house). Douglas stunned me by telling me that he and Tori were in love. Then he stood up, knocking over his chair, and asked to be taken back to his cell in case she called. Was it something I said? Something about my appearance? How could I have been so blind?

Now don't get me wrong, Ms. Spelling is a very beautiful and talented actress, but what could she offer him that I can't? His sudden change of affection to Tori from myself is clear-cut proof that he is greatly disturbed and is not ready to be released back into society.

Regretfully,

Linda Granger
"Victim"

P.S. I've been thinking of going red with my hair, since it's so "in" now. What do you think?

To Santos and the boys in the guard room— You can't incarcerate me anytime! Love, Linda.

THE GYPSY CAB COMPANY

CHIC ON CRIME

In the old country I run with a rough crowd, I walk in nightclub wearing a white suit. Somebody look at me funny, I walk out of club wearing red suit. And it wasn't my blood. Now I try to keep my nose on the straight and narrow. But the cab business is shit and New York is an expensive city. So I have a little action on the side. You want to buy a girl? How 'bout a missile, or plutonium ... half price this week, my friend.

H.R.H. ON CRIME

    PIP

Mr. Orenthal James Simpson, Your Highness.

    H.R.H.

We loved your television show last year. "Crime of the Century." Marvellously entertaining. However, I was terribly disappointed with the last episode. I wagered two hundred guineas in the palace pool that you would be hung, drawn, and quartered. Needless to say I lost. Did you get the idea for the plot from my ancestor, Henry the Eighth? He always got away with it, too. Oops, you seem to have dropped a glove. Good-bye.

Ms. Hope Finch
P.O. Box 1749, Taconic Pkwy.
Connecticut
E-mail@www.lenslady.edu

FEMALL CIRCUMCISION
"CUT IT OUT!"

HOPE FINCH ON CRIME

Well, a bunch of us were walking, and there was this dumpster, and next to it was this really pretty rug that was all rolled up. It looked kind of worn, but it was basically fine, so everyone decided to take it back to the dorm and maybe put it in the lounge so we could have a rug, you know?

So it was really heavy, and everyone helped carry it into the

lounge, and then someone unrolled it, and there was a dead body in it. Swear to G-d! It was this guy, and he'd been shot in the head and rolled up in the rug. Isn't that totally freaky? It really happened!

. . . I wasn't actually there, but my friend was, and she saw it.

CHAPTER
FIVE
FAMILY

TRACEY ULLMAN ON FAMILY

There is a wonderful little shop near where I live in London that is run by a very Dickensian-looking older couple. The walls are adorned with hundreds of heraldic shields, and coats of arms, representing families dating back to the tenth century. For a fee they will trace your ancestry. My daughter Mabel became intrigued with the prospect, so one day we entered this charming establishment. A bell rang above the old wooden door, and the rosy-cheeked proprietor looked up. "How can I help you young ladies?" he asked. Mabel said she would love to trace our family tree.

"Well, my dear," he said. "I'll need a few details, let's start with your mother's side. . . . What is your maiden name, Madam?"

"Ullman," I told him.

"Ah!" he said. "Is that Scandinavian?"

"No, Austrian, as far as I know, but that doesn't stop people thinking I'm Liv's daughter and sending me invitations to the Helsinki Poetry Festival."

"Well, would it be a name of Hebrew origin?" he ventured.

"No, I'm not Jewish, but don't tell anyone in show business that! Once the Eltham Jewish Pensioners asked me to their bingo night, saying, 'Tracey darling, we're not sure if you're Jewish, but you're so clever you must be!' And then a cousin in Krakow told me that my Polish grandmother was rumored to have converted to Catholicism in the '30s, so I might turn out to be a *secret* Jew like the American secretary of state, Madeleine Albright, wouldn't that be great!"

"Hmm," said the man. "Let's try your mother's side. . . ."

"Will we get a coat of arms?" interrupted Mabel. "I like the ones with wolves and drawbridges!"

"My mum's mum was a Penfold," I told him. "And her family were Romany Gypsies who ran a travelling fairground."

"Gypsies?" said the man, taking a brochure out of Mabel's hands.

"Yes, want to buy some lucky heather, darling?" I quipped. "Or maybe you want your knives sharpened?"

"Are we in the Doomsday Book?" asked Mabel.

"Any leads on your grandfather's side?" he said wearily.

"Oh yeah, the sailor Harry Hagstrum, or it might have been Hogstrum, we're not really sure."

"What do you mean, you're not really sure?"

"Well, when he found out that my gran was up the duff, he went back to his native Norway (or it might have been Sweden) rather sharpish!"

"Up the duff?" he looked puzzled.

I corrected myself, "My grandmother was 'with child.'" There was a pause.

"I'm quite a mixture, aren't I—a mongrel—a mutt, an English-speaking Aryan, transient, Viking, Jew." The Anglo-Saxon detective looked stumped. But Mabel was determined not to leave the shop empty-handed, and one thing my family is is nouveau riche, so he sold us a plain shield, and the kids designed our own coat of arms. It looks like this.

Bugge Manor (Since 1578)

Virginia Bugge
& Timothy Bugge
(M.P. for Greater Diddlesbury)
Bugge Manor
Wrencham Hollow
Diddlesbury

VIRGINIA BUGGE ON FAMILY

Of course, my father used to beat me. Just as his own father beat him, and his father before him beat him, and so on. In fact, the family crest is a whip and two buttocks. But times have changed, sadly, and now the only way you can get your children beaten is to send them away to a very expensive school. But at least it's done in a professional manner, by experts.

Grandmother Puts the Icing on Granddaughter's Donut

Scott Del Monte

for *The Valley View* . . . continuing his series about families.

It was still dark as I pulled into the parking lot of the Kristi Yamaguchi Ice Dome, at 4:34 A.M., but I was not the first to arrive. "Where you been, we are here twenty minute already!" exclaimed Mrs. Noh Nang Ning, an energetic Asian woman in her 70s, whose dedication to her granddaughter Kim's skating career has become a family

obsession. Kim was warming up, pulling her left leg over her right ear and wearing a sweatshirt with a big donut on it, informing us that she is sponsored by her grandmother's company, "Yankee Doodle Donuts," with smaller letters underneath the logo reading "no MSG." The old lady turned to me, proffering a paper bag, "Want a donut?" Ah! Perfect sustenance for a cold dark morning, I reached in and took out a frosted bear claw. "Now you give me one dollar," said this savvy business woman. "A dollar?" I sputtered, instantly regretting querying her. "You have trouble hearing? One dollar!" I reached for my wallet. "You want coffee as well? Case donut get stuck in

your throat, and you make noise like — aaaaaakkkkk!" She demonstrated loudly, spraying me with donut crumbs and powdered sugar.

Box on Street

I handed her twenty dollars and before she could make change, Kim skated up and told us that her coach had not shown up. "I be your coach!" declared Mrs. Noh Nang Ning. "I best coach, I make you winner, winner, winner!" And with a firm hand to the small of Kim's back, she pushed her out onto the ice, crying, "You practice, you bring back gold! Make you and me famous, then Grandma get donut franchise. You lose, you no come home!" I asked her if she thought that was appropriate encouragement for a child. "Good motivation!" she exclaimed. "Kids don't want to sleep in box on street — higher Kim! Get that leg higher! You want to disappoint dead ancestors!!" And at that moment Kim's outstretched leg, helped by a combination of her grandmother's voice and three jelly donuts, did indeed go high enough for her thick black hair to get hopelessly entangled with her skate blade.

You Don't Win, You Nothing . . .

By now other skaters had begun to arrive, and we were joined by twelve-year-old Karyl-Lyn Salko, Kim's main competition. Karyl-Lyn told me that she was thrilled to be the state champion but that winning wasn't everything and that she was just proud to be on the team. "Bullshit!" declared Mrs. Noh Nang Ning. "You don't win, you nothing!" Karyl looked taken aback, but suddenly Mrs. Noh Nang Ning's inscrutable features softened and she uttered the familiar phrase, "You want donut?" She chuckled, "Pay later, when ship come in." I began to wonder if I had misjudged this woman. After all, her

humble origins in the eastern province of Nofukluk, and eighteen hour workdays in her donut store might explain her abrupt manner, and disinterest in small talk.

Franchise in Toilet

Karyl explained that she was going to be an Olympic Gold medalist, so she was on a special sports diet and that donuts were definitely not included! "Aah, just one," Mrs. Noh Nang Ning cooed. "You very pretty, too pretty. All the boys like. You kind who get pregnant at fifteen, have two kids hanging on

skirt but skirt too short. Butt cold all the time. You have to join Ice-Capades to feed family. You gotta eat donut to get energy for ten shows a day. First you play Beauty,

then you play Beast. Then you get too fat they kick you out of show. You have to scrape ice from rink to make snow cone to sell in stand. Nobody want you, nobody love you, then you die! So skip heartbreak, have donut now," said Mrs. Noh Nang Ning softly, pressing a chocolate donut into Karyl's open mouth. Pandora's box of donuts had certainly been opened. The young champion not only finished them but licked all the sprinkles off the bottom of the box and was soon taken to the hospital suffering from sugar shock. But, the feisty grandmother did not notice; she had turned her attentions back to the ice. "Kim, don't spin so fast! Donut logo on back going round too quickly, no one can read, franchise in toilet!" "Come on, Donut girl! You winner, winner, winner!"

Footnote: Since this article went to press, Kim has placed second in The Pan Pacific Panasonic Pageant, and, after a failed attack on a fellow competitor with a sharpened skate blade, Karyl-Lyn Salko has entered an eating disorder clinic.

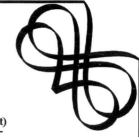

Trevor Ayliss
& Barrington LeTissier
Willows Mews Cottage
Osterly on the Green
Middlesex, MD12 6HE

(Come off the M40 at the Robin Hood Roundabout)

TREVOR AYLISS ON FAMILY

Dear Michael,

I've asked your mother to give you this letter when you're old enough to understand. Considering what I'm about to tell you, I'm hoping she waited 'til you were 45 or so! Ha, ha! Just having you on there. I'm a little nervous. Barry always says I make jokes when I'm nervous. I'll explain about Barry later. Anyway, you deserve to know where you came from.

My name is Trevor Michael Ayliss. Notice the middle name there, same as yours. Oh, I just had a lovely thought. Maybe by the time you read this, we'll already know each other! That would be quite nice. Perhaps you know me as your Uncle Trevor who comes round for dinner now and then and gives you extravagant gifts on your birthdays. Or as your mother's artistic

and stylish friend who cheers just a little bit too loudly at the wrong moments in your football matches. Perhaps we're pals by now, you and me. That would be grand.

But mates tell each other the truth, don't they, son? And the truth is, in a biological sort of way, I'm your dad. Has your mother explained to you all about biology? If not, there's a wonderful old picture you can rent called *Stella Dallas*, with Barbara Stanwyck, that will explain a lot.

So there it is. Your mother wanted to have you in the worst way, and I just helped her a bit. So I am your dad, but not really. Maybe by now Lianne's found a man to fill those shoes. I've got a life of my own with a man named Barry. But don't think I don't care about you, son, because I do. And if I can ever do anything for you—if you need help with travel arrangements or you're confused on when to wear seersucker, I'm your man. Also I got a look at you in the nursery this morning, and I see you've inherited the Ayliss feet—high insteps and weak ankles. Ever so sorry about that. Get yourself some good arch supports and don't set your sights on a career in dance. Heartbreak waits there. I know.

Be good to your mother, Michael. She loves you very much.

Yours,

Trevor Ayliss

ROSENTHAL PHARMACIES

(at 17 brightly lit locations)

FERN ROSENTHAL ON FAMILY

Harry and I have been shopping for a condo at the Beau Rivage. . . .

Oh, Harry tells me it's Mirage. Whatever darling, a condo complex in Boca Raton. We looked at hundreds of floor plans, and we decided to go for one without a family room. And suddenly, I started to cry. I said, "Harry, I just realized that we don't need a family room because we're not a family anymore." "You want a family?" he said. "I'll buy you a dog. One of those Lhasa Shitzus." What, is he nuts? We just ordered white carpeting.

Wimpman, KROSS, and Wussman
"You name it, we'll sue it." *(Since 1987)*
PENTHOUSE
F. LEE BAILEY LEGAL CENTER
100 CANON DRIVE
BEVERLY HILLS

FROM THE COMMAND STATION OF SYDNEY KROSS

You show me a family, and I'll show you dysfunction! I'll show you the roots of sexual deviance, the seeds of violence, and the germs of dishonesty!

✔ Your mother was a lovely woman?
  She smothered you with affection until you gasped for breath!

✔ Your father was a wonderful role model?
  He set a standard too high to reach, which made you feel inadequate and weak!

✔ Your siblings were marvelous?
  They obstructed all of your opportunities to grow and thrive as an independent entity.

✔ Your aunts and uncles were negative influences, your cousins traumatized you, and your grandparents were a recurring embarrassment!

But don't get me wrong. I love and support the family unit wholeheartedly — they are the bedrock of my entire defense practice.

"I'LL TUMBLE FOR YA!"

RAYLEEN GIBSON
Professional Stuntwoman &
Chief Executive Officer of AAAH
(Aged Animal Actor's Home)

RAYLEEN GIBSON ON FAMILY

Mitch and I'll probably have some little brats one day, although he's worried about walking around with a three-year-old who's taller than he is. But in the meantime, I'm not taking any chances: I use the cap, Mitch has his condoms, I'm on the pill, I got a coil fitted, and I'm thinking of having security cameras installed, just to stop him from sneaking up on me while I'm asleep, the little bugger!

VAN NUYS SAVINGS & LOAN

KAY CLARK.
ASSISTANT BRANCH MANAGER

KAY CLARK ON FAMILY

It's always been just Mother and me. I remember the last time I saw my father; it was just after the accident in Piccadilly Circus. "I didn't know the damn motorbike would part company with the sidecar, Mildred," he shouted over his shoulder, as he sped off up Shaftesbury Avenue. And later, I remember the cold, steely glint in Mother's eye as she stared up at me from her iron lung. "Kay," she said, "don't ever marry. All men will try to kill you after they've done nasty things to your downstairs areas." Now only family could be that protective of you.

A LARK WITH KAY CLARK

YOU KNOW YOU'RE IN TROUBLE WHEN YOUR COMPUTER HAS MORE MEMORY THAN YOU DO!

cogito, ergo sum.

RUBY ROMAINE ON FAMILY

I come from a big family. I don't mean a lot of brothers and sisters. I mean my mother and father were big . . . fat. Fat as a house, both of them. My family is from Wisconsin, and just about everything I ever saw any of them put in their mouths had milk, butter, or cheese in it. Made for funny breath, too.

When we moved to California we lived in a trailer out in North Hollywood . . . that was when it was filled with orange groves instead of taco stands, if you know what I mean. And growing up with two 300-pounders in a tiny trailer is no picnic. My room was basically whatever space was left after they sat down.

And boy, when that old sun used to beat down on that aluminum roof and my folks were inside, I swear you could smell their fat frying. My dad used to keep the front door open, and sometimes they would sweat so much one of them would slide right out the door onto our Astroturf lanai.

CHAPTER
SIX
MONEY

TRACEY ULLMAN ON MONEY

I couldn't wait to start earning money. Money is freedom. My first job was when I was fourteen. I helped out on Saturdays at a local bakers' and earned about $4.00 for the day. But I had a problem with this job; I found it impossible to put the delicious cream cakes that we sold into bags without licking the excess off my fingers. The manageress, who had hair like a peroxide helmet, warned me on a number of occasions to stop being so unhygienic, but I couldn't control my reflex. So they handed me a bag of broken biscuits in exchange for my pink nylon overall, and I headed for the Kings Road, where I found a job selling jeans.

I now earned $8.00 plus commission. I was desperate for that commission; extra money meant being able to buy a round of Harvey Wallbangers for my friends in the pub. This was 1976, and people wore their bellbottoms skintight. I could get a flabby, white-thighed size 14 dolly bird into a pair of size 8 Levi's, by lying her on the floor and pulling up the zipper with a wire coat hanger. Admittedly the customer couldn't breathe, walk, or talk in them, and occasionally the hanger slipped and I gave them an appendectomy. But they usually bought the jeans because the thought of trying to get them off again was too overwhelming, and I made an extra buck.

Then I left school and started full-time employment. I got a job with a paper products distribution company for 40 pounds a week. A fortune! I was in an office full of men in white nylon shirts who smoked pipes and played cricket at the weekends. Everybody spoke in hushed tones and lived for the moment that the tea trolley arrived at 3 P.M. One day I found a pornographic magazine in the boss's desk drawer. It didn't disgust me; it gave me hope that someone was alive in this place. I stuck it out until

I got a job as a dancer in a summer show at a British seaside re-
sort. When I told the personnel officer I was leaving, she was
flabbergasted. "How can you do this, Tracey?" You would have
thought I was off to the Middle East as a white sex slave. "You're
earning good money here," she said. "And in five years time you
might get Carol's job!" Carol wore a white nylon dress and
earned 60 pounds a week.

Well, I'm glad I took the plunge. The years have passed and
I'll be honest, a fair deal of money has come my way, and I appreciate every penny. And now I can buy all the bloody cream
cakes I want! And I do, and stuff my face with them, until I burst
out of my designer jeans!

RUBY ROMAINE ON MONEY

Y'know, this is a lousy country. As Bette Davis told me once, "getting old ain't for sissies," and now I know what she meant. It's tough. People don't want to hire you. Money becomes a problem. I'm supposed to get by on my Social Security, my union pension, and Buddy's disability that the Army sends him every month. Hell, I can't even afford a pet, unless you count Buddy. . . .The other day when I tried to pay for my groceries, the checkout girl said to me that I couldn't purchase liquor and cigarettes with food stamps. Like I said, it's a lousy country!

"I'LL TUMBLE FOR YA!"

RAYLEEN GIBSON
Professional Stuntwoman &
Chief Executive Officer of AAAH
(Aged Animal Actor's Home)

RAYLEEN GIBSON ON MONEY

I can't work forever as a stuntperson. Eventually the body'll give out, and I'll have to quit. So I've got myself a few other financial irons in the fire, for when that day comes. The best one is a new line of all-natural Australian cosmetics that I make myself. I make a super sunscreen from liquefied koala stool. I grind it up in the blender and get a nice faeces frapp. It has naturally digested eucalyptus in it, so it smells refreshing, and you get about a number-fifteen protection. I also make a good hair conditioner from certain parts of the wombat mixed with tea tree oil. It's very healthy, inexpensive, and if you like cats, it draws 'em right to you like a magnet. All that's left now is getting a celebrity endorsement. I wrote to Nicole Kidman and Elle McPherson—I wanted to give first crack to my fellow countrymen—but I never heard back. Stuck up bitches. That's all right. No problem. When Mitch and I open our other business—Celebrity Bodyguards — we'll become known as the best in town. Those two bitches'll come beggin' for help when they get a stalker or something, and I'll just smile and say, "Sorry, too busy—and your hair looks like shit."

H.R.H. ON MONEY

PIP
Shaquille O'Neal, Your Highness.

H.R.H.
Oh. I've never heard of you, but Pip tells me you put balls through hoops and get paid an inordinate amount of money. While you are in my country, maybe you'd like to make a sound investment in a British title. I believe the Earldom of Egham is available. You'll get two plowed fields near Runnymede, tickets to Wimbledon, and right to deflower virgins on midsummer's eve. Just make the check payable to me. Good-bye.

THE FAMILY SPENDING WEB SITE

LINDA GRANGER ON MONEY

Fawn Loving: Hi there, and welcome to the Family Spending Web site. Well, today could not be more specialer or fantastically exciting because today, this glorious day for logging on and shopping, we have got my dear, good friend Miss Lisa Granger. . . .

Linda Granger: That's Linda, dear.

Fawn Loving: Sorry, that was a type O. Miss Linda Granger. Welcome back. As you know, last time Linda was on-line with us here, she was here to be here with her book, *I'm Still Here.*

Linda Granger: That's right Fawn. And that happy experience led me to create my new Recovery Dolls—each one of them marks a milestone of survival in my life. May I show you, Fawn?

Fawn Loving: That would be marvelously good.

Linda Granger: First we have Little Loopy Linda, representing my alcoholic period. As you can see, the eyes are slightly crossed and there are little hand-painted flecks of vomit on the cheek and chin, and running down the dress.

Fawn Loving: I hope you folks at home can see on your screens exactly how carefully crafted with careful craftsmanship these dolls are crafted.

Linda Granger: Now this one is Druggy Dear, representing my descent into hell during my drug addiction period when I attempted suicide several times. You can see the hand-stitched scars on the wrists —and it has a removable stomach that can be pumped by any child.

Fawn Loving: Educational is a wonderful thing.

Linda Granger: Also, if you tilt its little head its eyeballs vanish. You know, my friends call this one Barbiturate Barfie.

Fawn Loving: I love that! (LOL) And then this one comes in an Afro-American version I understood I was told.

Linda Granger: We're not biased. Black people have drug problems, too. So we decided to go right ahead and make one just for them.

Fawn Loving: So marvelously inclusive. Okay, let's go right to the Virtual Store, where all you Virtual shoppers are waiting in virtuality. Hello, Family Spender . . .

Trevor: *Hello, Miss Granger. My name is Trevor. I saw you in Vegas a few months ago. You were stunning and I want to buy your doll.*

Linda Granger: Well, aren't you sweet. Which one would you like?

Trevor: *I want the set. I'm giving them to my — uh — lover.*

Linda Granger: And what's <u>his</u> name?

Trevor: *It's that obvious, is it? Even on the Internet?*

Linda Granger: Sweetheart, when you've been a fag hag as long as I have you know right away. Your font was a giveaway. Now, Trevor, will this be a gift?

Trevor: *Yes, it's for my companion, Barry — it's to celebrate Cole Porter's <u>birthday.</u>*

Fawn Loving: Wonderful, all right, I'm going to take another Web shopper, shall we? Hello.

WaynesWrld: *Hiya, this is Ruby Romaineeee from North Hollywood.*

Fawn Loving: You're welcome to the Family Spending Channel. Are you a regular family spender?

WaynesWrld: *My grandson Wayne logs on for me a couple of times a year when I've had a fewwww too many. I sent back a marconite necklace. It was a goddammmmm piece of coal on a wire.*

Linda Granger: Which doll would you like, dear? Are you a collector?

WaynesWrld: *Nah, this is for my little great-grandchild, Linda. But I kind of gottaaaa problem 'cause Karen, that's my granddddaughter, she married a black guy and the child—well, she's the cutest little thing you could ever see—but she's kind of beige, so I don't know if I should get a black or a white doll.*

Fawn Loving: May I suggest one of each?

WaynesWrld: *You may suggest a champagne colonic, but I ain't spending that kind of money.*

Fawn Loving: All right, dear spender; I'll turn you over to an operator who will help you select your selection. And we'll be right back, after a page break, with Sex Addict Linda . . .

Linda Granger: She has bendable knees!

PRIVATE CHAT ROOM

Linda: How much have I made? How am I doin'?

Fawn: Super well—not as good as Patty Duke's motivational tapes but better than Ed Asner's skin cream.

Linda: I need this money for back surgery.

Fawn: Oh, come on. Aren't all those hard luck stories just to sell merchandise products?

FAMSPEND.CON BULLETIN: *Our services have temporarily been interrupted. There has been a sizable earthquake that was epicentered at the Lompock Industrial Park, California. Please wait for server connection . . .*

BACK ON-LINE . . .

Fawn Loving: Friends, we've had some earthquake—nothing to stop your spending, but unfortunately Miss Granger has been struck by a falling bookcase and is currently pinned to her keyboard beneath ten boxes of unsold wrenches. . . . Oh, she's trying to type something. . . . Oh, what a trooper.

Linda Granger: I wIll be back IΛΙ two weEKs wITII a little concussion doΛ witH a steel plate in its head....

PRIVATE CHAT ROOM

Linda: Fowɴ, I thInk oNe of *my* breΛSt implants Ħas rupTurEd, i can feel the sillΘon leɑking IᴫΤo my cheℼt cavity.

IRS FIELD REPORT

Agent: Tom Hart (#7177)

Name: Mr. Chic Avi Avava . . .
(Please verify. Second
name obscured by HOT SEX sticker)

Job Description: Cab Driver

POLICE DEPARTMENT

NEW YORK CITY
TRANSIT AUTHORITY

EXPIRES MARCH

CHIC AVA
(NAME   ER)

HOT SEX

DRIVER'S NUMBER

670

NOTICE TO PASSENGERS — Keep a record
of the above name and number on this card.

U. F. 39-D   POLICE COMMISSIONER.

I was unable to contact the above by letter
or telephone so I hailed his cab as he left the depot. The following is a transcript
of the interview, as recorded by the standard MP4-21 field wire I employed. I
apologize for the unnatural peaks of velocity reached on this recording. Please
play at low level.

Agent Hart: Okay, Mr. Avab . . . Avan . . . Ava . . .

Mr. Chic: Chic! Please call me this. Everybody know me because I'm a
chick magnet. You like chicks? What you say we forget this whole
tax audit bullshit, and I get you laid.

Agent Hart: Mr. Chic I work for the IRS and . . .

Mr. Chic: Oh, that's right, so you're just here to f-ck me, right my friend?

Agent Hart: We're just here to find out the truth, and what seems apparent to
us is that you have grossly overstated your deduction entitlements
on form BS102 lines 14 through 28—excluding line 22e.

Mr. Chic: I forget. What was 22e?

Agent Hart: I've just decided to allow the deduction for the five cases of auto
interior fresheners. Could you crack open a new one? [This guy
stank!]

Mr. Chic: Surely! No problem! I have very cherry, lotsa lemon. Here, take
some for yourself.

[sound of packaged air fresheners striking on and around hidden mike]

Agent Hart:	These can be construed as a bribe. Now let's have a looksee at some of these so-called business write-offs. Three hundred dollars at Raffi's House of Fine Suedes and Leathers?
Mr. Chic:	It's for my uniform, Raffi gives me a deal. You know how much aborted lambskins cost retail? Here feel for yourself, please.
Agent Hart:	Okay, I'll allow that. But the real red flag for us is the $5,217.00 you claim for charitable donations. I need to see receipts, sir.
Mr. Chic:	What the f-ck receipts? You think homeless people give receipts? I buy the Girl Scouts' cookies, I throw money in the "Make a Wish" fountain. I make a lot of wishes for a better world . . . and what do I get? . . . The IRS breathing down my pants!
Agent Hart:	Well, Mr. Chic, I'm afraid the IRS can't accept your unaccounted-for generosity.
Mr. Chic:	They are shit bags we should push them into the sea! Except for you my friend, I give to you little floaty wings, now what can you do for me?
Agent Hart:	I can accept cash, check, or money orders for the sum total of . . .

[During the following you can hear a loud banging noise—the sound of Mr. Chic's head repeatedly making contact with the Perspex partition.]

Agent Hart:	. . . $1,573.22. We must be in receipt of this payment within thirteen working days, or you will be arrested and your assets seized pending trial.

[horn honking]

[random cursing and groaning]

Mr. Chic:	Why is it always me! My piece of shit brother, he tells me, "It's okay, Chic, go ahead, hide your tips as donation, nobody check this stuff, I do it all the time," and the falafel business is good. He makes three times what I do!
Agent Hart:	If your brother is indeed defrauding the government, it's your patriotic duty to turn him in. And if your information proves to be accurate, you will receive a cash reward.

Mr. Chic: Really? This is very interesting to me, my friend. [Sticks his head out of the window] Hey! F-ck you, salami head!

[sound of tires screeching heavily]

Mr. Chic: Let's go!

[The next five minutes contains no dialogue, just screams, shifting thuds from the passenger cabin, curses, and a police siren, as we proceeded to a new locale, "Piki's Falafel a la Carte" on 34th and Tenth—an independently owned, portable eatery.] Dialogue resumes:

Mr. Piki: You turn your own brother in, you camel f-cker!!

Mr. Chic: Mr. Hart, don't forget to check the baba ganoush, he hides his gold coins in there!

[The squelching sounds are of me, elbow deep in a tub of Piki's Carte Special.]
[sound of a knife being sharpened]

Mr. Piki: I will slice you like Shishlick!

Mr. Chic: Shishlick my dick, brother!

[rapidly retreating footsteps]

Mr. Piki: Eh, my friend, what you looking here, this is small tomatoes. My cousin Momo, he has rug business, he makes six times what I make!

Mr. Piki then led me to his cousin Momo, on the corner of 4th and Broadway, who was selling shag-pile carpet from the back of a blue Vista Cruiser. Mr. Momo, when questioned, became irate and offered me the name of "a really big fish in the sea," a Mr. Sabi who operates out of Sabi's Videos on Queens Boulevard. . . .

IMPORTANT NOTE: Requesting at least twelve more field agents, I think I've unearthed something big here. . . .

The Tara Estates
"A Gated & Graceful Community"
Birdie Godsen

BIRDIE GODSEN ON MONEY

I never worry about money. Robert has total job security at his company — he's very high up in the tobacco industry. Between a generous salary package and a highly competitive bonus system, we're very comfortable. The minute he signed the Loyalty Oath and the Non-Freedom of Information Contract, the money just started pouring in. One time CBS called (that colored gentleman with an earring from the *60 Minutes* program), Robert said that he had "no comment." The next day, the company issued him a bonus check for two thousand dollars! It's very satisfying for Robert to be appreciated for all his hard work. And it's so nice having him home during the week. They gave him two whole months paid vacation. It's part of a new incentive program called "We Hear You." They put little tiny microphones in every room of the house, and as long as Robert doesn't talk to anyone from the government or the media, he can do whatever he wants. Right now he's building a life-size model of a human lung out of cheesecloth and popsicle sticks in our rec room. He burns several pounds of tobacco in that lung every day, and it's darkened somewhat, but it's <u>never</u> gotten a tumor. It may be bonus time again!

CHAPTER
SEVEN
SEX

TRACEY ULLMAN ON SEX

I have no problem talking about sex when I'm dressed up as a character. I played Linda Granger as a nymphomaniac, flashing her zebra print panties and slobbering all over a fellow actor. I play Chic the hairy cabbie, who boasts about the size of his organ and how any woman who has sex with him becomes his slave. In fact, I am so confident and convincing as Chic that women on the set of my show threaten to leave their husbands! But when I take off the wigs and glue and become Tracey again, I have nothing in public to say about my own sex life, absolutely nothing!!!

A doctor friend of mine in San Diego is a sex therapist. She gives counseling and performs surgery, such as inserting penile pumps for impotent men. She talks very fondly of one guy called Ted who received one of these aids and is very willing to show other prospective clients how it works. She tells me that she calls him up, explains that someone's a little trepidacious, and he says cheerfully, "We're there!" making his penis sound as if it's the other half of a vaudeville act. "He gets it out in front of anyone," she says, "pumps it up and down as many times as you want, shows you where he screws on the bulb, he loves it!" Now there's someone with no inhibitions about his sexuality! An inspiration to us all, surely? But I can't help thinking that maybe Ted has taken away a tad of the mystique and allure about himself—so I think I'll remain silent.

Wimpman, KROSS, and Wussman
"You name it, we'll sue it." (Since 1987)
PENTHOUSE
F. LEE BAILEY LEGAL CENTER
100 CANON DRIVE
BEVERLY HILLS

FROM THE COMMAND STATION OF SYDNEY KROSS

Men can't see me as a sexual being, but I'm just like any other woman. I have needs, desires. I have time between meetings. The last three men I've been with were impotent. Can you believe it? Three noodles in a row. One guy ran out of my house with his pants down just because I strapped on a normal-sized dildo. Then there was the guy whose "magic wand" flopped when I told him his penis was cute. And how can I forget Larry, who got furious just because I was writing notes ... on him, during foreplay. I don't know what I'm doing wrong. Maybe it's the stigma of being voted "The Girl You'd Least Like to Have a Blow Job By" in law school. That really hurt.

POLICE INCIDENT REPORT

DATE: 12/6/96

CONDUCTED BY: SGT. COLE

THE FOLLOWING IS A TRANSCRIPT OF MY INTERVIEW WITH A MS. RUBY ROMAINE, CONDUCTED AT 23:48 HOURS, REGARDING AN ENCOUNTER WITH AN EXTRATERRESTRIAL.

SGT. COLE: Name?

ROMAINE: Ruby Romaine . . . like the lettuce.

SGT. COLE: And what seems to be the trouble, Ms. Romaine?

ROMAINE: Well, Officer, I had a strange encounter I thought I better report to the authorities.

SGT. COLE: Go ahead.

ROMAINE: Well, I had stopped off at my favorite watering hole down on Ventura Boulevard for a few splashes. . . .
    As I left I told my friend Gerry to keep it in his pants, as I always do [chuckles]. Then I got in my Buick and drove back over the hill, lit myself a Pall Mall, and played a little champagne music on the tape player . . . I had a fling once with Lawrence Welk.

SGT. COLE: That's irrelevant.

ROMAINE: It wasn't to Mrs. Welk. Anyhoo . . . I went up Coldwater

Canyon and turned left on Mulholland. The Valley is beautiful that time of night, with the twinkling lights and all. . . . I was enjoying the drive when all of a sudden I was blinded by a very bright light that kind of just exploded in front of me. Then the car started trembling and honking its horn. I climbed out to see what was causing such a howdee doo . . . and then I saw him. He was short and squat with big black eyes and he sort of came outta the light.

At this point I asked Ms. Romaine to draw, to the best of her abilities, the alleged alien:

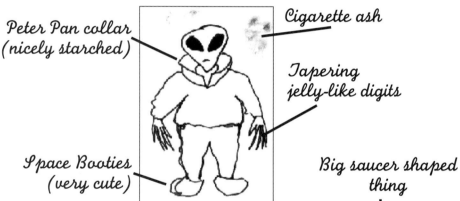

Peter Pan collar
(nicely starched)

Cigarette ash

Tapering
jelly-like digits

Space Booties
(very cute)

Big saucer shaped
thing

ROMAINE (*cont.*): I says to him, "What's going on? Are you one of those alien people?" Then he took my hand and led me into the light. I was kind of trepidacious at first, but I followed his little flippered feet over to a ramp that led up to this big saucer-shaped thing.

Once we got inside, everything was like aluminum, only bathed in a phosphorescent glow. Little Greenie offered me a drink, always an icebreaker with me. Whatever it was, I got a hell of a buzz out of it. Must have been moonshine. I looked around, and you know what? He had a lovely home. I noticed a picture of a tall green guy hanging on the wall.

Tall green guy. A real lounge lizard, a cross between Gene Barry and a cucumber.

He was standing next to some kind of flag or pennant. I guess he was the top alien back home, the mayor of the moon or whatever.

Anyhoo, I turned around and there he was, the alien fella from the snapshot, stepping out of this dumbwaitergizmo. Then the little gherkin began to play some kind of weird organ music and I got the feeling big boy wanted to dance. It looked like he was trying for a cha cha cha or a rumba. So we tripped the light fantastic for a while and worked up to quite a warp factor! We had a couple more of those drinky things, and eventually I wound up on this aluminum Barcalounger. . . .

Then he began to probe my galaxy! And boy! He went where no man's gone before . . . and right at the tail end of things his ass lit up like a blowtorch!

Glowing Ass

ROMAINE (*cont.*): Later Little Greenie walked me back to my car. And you know something? While I was gone it had been washed and Simonized! Then he goes back up the ramp, gets into the spaceship, and whoosh! It was gone.

SGT. COLE: Yeah. Tell me, do you have some evidence of their existence? Did they give you anything?

ROMAINE: Not even a hickey!

SGT. COLE: Ms. Romaine, regulations require that I ask you this question.

ROMAINE: Okay.

SGT. COLE: Are you sure that this was not a fantasy, that you didn't just dream the whole thing?

ROMAINE: Look, I know you have to ask these questions because this is a high-level investigation, right? But no. As sure as God made little green apples, this was one hundred percent real!

SGT. COLE: I see. Well, don't worry about a thing. First thing in the morning I'll take care of this.

ROMAINE: Okeydokey. This could be quite a career booster for you.

SGT. COLE: Oh, that'd be great.

I then escorted Ms. Romaine out of the station, and as she fumbled with the clublock on her steering wheel, something bizarre happened. Now maybe it was the combination of the static on her polyester pants, it being four in the morning, and me having had seven cups of coffee, but I swear that just for a second, Ms. Romaine's ass lit up and pulsated. Whatever it was, I think this incident requires further investigation.

VIRGINIA BUGGE ON SEX

Who's in and who's out . . .

with the home counties' own Camilla Parkington-Bowlesford

MP'S WIFE, VIRGINIA BUGGE, SPEAKS OUT ON HER HUSBAND'S GAY SEX SCANDAL

I'll admit it, Timmy did once have a sexual incident with a chap. It was at school. In the music room. While everyone else was out on a cross-country run. It was a sort of . . . touching thing. The point is —and I can't stress this enough—while it was happening he was *thinking* of a woman. Julie Christie. All Timmy's dorm were at the time.

And I think, even if something happens with a chap, as long as you're thinking of a woman, then you're not a homosexualist. Not in my book. And I can honestly say, on his behalf, that he's never thought of a man during sex. . . . Except when we were engaged and he thought my father might barge in and find us doing it on the billiard table. But this purported incident in the House of Commons Chapel is absaballylutely . . .

(*continued on page 31*)

VAN NUYS SAVINGS & LOAN

KAY CLARK
ASSISTANT BRANCH MANAGER

KAY CLARK ON SEX

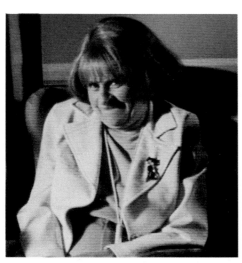

"S-E-X?" What's there to say, really? Mother must've told me a thousand times: "If you let a man touch your downstairs region, you'll regret it for the rest of your life." She was right in a way. I had to get a pap smear and a pelvic exam last year. Oh, dear. I became rather agitated, what with mother's words playing over and over in my head. I'm afraid the exam took an hour or two longer than expected. And even with the two tranquilizer tablets they gave me, the doctor complained that I cut off the circulation in his wrist. I said I was sorry! I just tensed up. I'd still be willing to give it a try some day, though. "S-E-X," I mean. With a nice, understanding man, not on a hard table with a spotlight on me and a nurse shouting at me to relax. I'd still take the tranquilizers though, and the poster on the ceiling of the kitty saying, "Hang in there!" They were nice.

> ### A LARK WITH KAY CLARK
> "AS SOON AS YOU FIND THE KEY TO SUCCESS, SOMEBODY ALWAYS CHANGES THE LOCK!"

Ms. Hope Finch
P.O. Box 1749, Taconic Pkwy.
Connecticut
E-mail@www.lenslady.edu

P.A.P.T.I.C.
People Against Pediatric Tobacco
Inhalation and Combustion

"Kick Joe Camel in the Butt!"

HOPE FINCH ON SEX

Even though I'm a virgin, I know what I'm gonna be doing, sexually speaking, for the rest of my life. By the time I get my bachelor's degree, I'm going to have a boyfriend who is intense and romantic. Since he's going to be my first man ever, he's going to have some, but not a lot of, experience. By the time I meet him, he will have had an affair with a very careful nurse who taught him how to make love.

Then, the summer before grad school, I'm going to let myself fall wildly in love with a man who can't make a living. Since he won't be working, he will have time to make love to me night and day, so I'm going to get addicted to his penis.

I'll have to choose between supporting him and my education. I'm going to choose my education.

My first deep love will be when I get a job in journalism. He will be my mentor. And I'll love him more than he loves me. The sex will be Tarrantino-ish. And he'll probably die while on foreign assignment.

In my grief, I'll throw myself into my work. And when I'm well established, I'll meet the man I want to marry. The sex will be good and animalistic at first. Then it will wane. My orgasms will go from explosions to humming. The explosions will come back when we go on tropical vacations. . . .

And then . . .

[I'll finish this after my Bolivian Tribal Dance class]

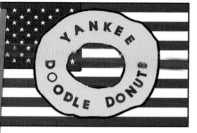

YANKEE
DOODLE DONUTS

"EVERY DAY FRESHIN'"

MRS. NOH NANG NING ON SEX

WHEN I COME TO AMERICA I ALMOST VIRGIN. THEN I GO TO LAS VEGAS AND I GO TO BIG SHOW. I SEE FAMOUS SINGER. I NOT TELL NAMES. HE SINGER WHO IS SHORT WITH BIG HEAD. NOW YOU KNOW WHO I MEAN. I DECIDE THAT HE IS MAN AND A HALF, WHICH NUNANG NEEDS. I THROW HOTEL KEY ON STAGE AND IT HIT HIM IN EYE. HE NOTICE ME. AFTER SHOW, HE INVITE ME TO ROOM. WE TAKE OFF CLOTHES AND GET ON WATER BED WHICH IS MOVING, MOVING. REMIND ME OF HOW I SNEAK INTO AMERICA. IT VERY GOOD SEX. NOW I UNDERSTAND WHY EVERYONE IN MOVIE IS SAYING OOOH, AHHH, YES. YES. YES! WHEN IT ALL OVER, HE GIVE ME FIVE HUNDRED DOLLAR. THIS MAKE ME ASHAMED BECAUSE HE THINK I AM HOOKER. . . . WHERE I COME FROM, WHORES ARE CARRIED THROUGH STREET AND TAKEN TO RIVER WHERE THEY ARE SET ON FIRE. . . . I WANT TO SAY THIS IS NOT BUSINESS BETWEEN US, BUT COULD NOT FIND WORDS. ONLY WORDS I COULD SPEAK WAS TO ASK BIG-HEADED SINGER IF HE WANT SEX AGAIN. HE SAY "YES." GIVE ME ANOTHER FIVE HUNDRED DOLLAR. PAY FOR WHOLE TRIP!

RAYLEEN GIBSON ON SEX

Dear Penthouse Forum,

I'm sure you're aware that this is not the first time I've written to you bastards! Bloody hell, for your star letter last month you chose some stupid jerk talkin' about shaggin' the babysitter. Like that's really original! I can't understand why you won't print me and my Mitch's sexcapades; is it because he's a little person? Mitch may be small but he's got a whanger like a king kangaroo, and I've sent the photos to prove it! So let me remind you of our

cutting edge, crossing-the-sexual-frontiers experiences. You see, as stunt people, we feel the adrenaline rush of danger every day — so, horizontal in the bedroom with Kris Kristofferson on the hi-fi just didn't send us where we wanted to go, even with the lava lamp on, so we started experimenting.

Our first sexcapade was in the movie *Passenger 57*. We joined the mile-high club on that one. But, hey, not in the latrine — that's for amateurs! You know the part where Wesley Snipes pins the terrorist down in his seat with a gun to his head? If you listen real close, you can hear a thumpin' sound. That's us doin' the nasty in the overhead compartment. I don't recommend that one unless you're lucky like me and your lover is under official carry-on size. Also, in *Jurassic Park* when that glass of water starts to shake in the jeep? Boom. Boom. That's Mitch here bangin' my pink bass drum whilst we're hangin' from the drive train. Mr. Spielberg claimed the credit on that one!

But we've had our failures, too. Like on *Apollo 13* we tried doin' it in the weightless environment. But we found out the hard way, you need gravity to get the job done. I mean, how can I put it? There's like no friction in space. And it's kind of disconcerting seeing your partner's sperm floating by.

But on our last gig, the new James Bond movie, 007 uses

this hang glider to land on an aircraft carrier out in the bay. But we had other ideas for that contraption! Like two very large insatiable pelicans, we came together in an orgy of flight. The wind was our brother—friction our friend . . .

P.S. If you don't print this, I'll shove my head up a dead bear's ass. Now that's an idea you jerks would probably print!

The Tara Estates
"A Gated & Graceful Community"
Birdie Godsen

BIRDIE GODSEN ON SEX

As a concerned parent, I believe sex education is better taught at home than in the schools. For instance, one day my ten-year-old, Christopher, came back from his Christian Youth Wilderness Hunting Weekend, just stuffed full of stories about werewolves, vampires, and Jews. And his first night back, he woke up from a nightmare screaming, "Mother, I'm going to be a wolfman! Mother, I'm going to be a blood sucker!" So, I sat him down calmly and explained that the only way he could grow so much extra hair and turn himself into a werewolf was if he touched himself in a certain dirty way. I thereby headed off a sexual abomination at the pass. But, just in case, I tied the mittens of his sleep suit together real tight that night.

CHAPTER EIGHT
FAME

TRACEY ULLMAN ON FAME

I had no idea I'd be famous, but an incident that occurred in 1973 gave me some hope. I was thirteen years old, and at that time we lived beside the river Thames in a house that was up for sale. Someone knocked on the door one Sunday morning and I hesitated to answer it, because on a previous occasion I had let in a woman who asked to use the toilet. It wasn't till she was halfway up the stairs that I'd realised she was a bag lady. She then locked herself in the bathroom and not only proceeded to use the loo but also took a shower, shampooed her hair, and shaved her legs before my stepfather could force the lock. My sister had teased me mercilessly about my lack of judgement, so this time I opened the door just a crack and checked for plastic carrier bags and the smell of beer. I found a very respectable couple on the doorstep, who asked politely if the house was still for sale. I called for my mother, and she arrived and proceeded to give them details. Suddenly the woman, who had been staring at me intently, interrupted her, saying, "Before you go any further, I must tell you that your daughter has an enormous star over her head." I was very surprised by this and quickly looked at myself in the hall mirror to see if I could see it. "I am a clairvoyant," she explained, "and can see these things. She will be famous, and have great success, especially in America." My mother smiled politely and in her usual commonsensical way said, "Oh, I know that! Can't you tell me how much I'm going to sell this house for?"

My sister teased me mercilessly about this, too, but now I get the last laugh. I've often thought about that lady, and wherever she is, I would like to thank her for giving a mousy, flat-chested teenager with a big nose some hope as she headed into the great unknown.

Wimpman, KROSS, and Wussman
"You name it, we'll sue it." (Since 1987)
PENTHOUSE
F. LEE BAILEY LEGAL CENTER
100 CANON DRIVE
BEVERLY HILLS

FROM THE COMMAND STATION OF SYDNEY KROSS

Lawyers used to be people who facilitated the law in nice suits. Occasionally one would speak to the press on behalf of a celebrity client. That was it. Low profile. Now, in the wake of "the trial," lawyers are celebrities. They're sitting behind Jack Nicholson at the Lakers game. They have tables by the window at Spago and get photographed by Annie Leibowitz. Fame has come to the legal profession, but we still have our advantage over everyone else.... We get to bill for our fifteen minutes.

The Craziest Thing I Ever Did!

Felix "Flip" Lazar

*C*harles *"Candy" Casino is still a superagent after forty-six years in the business. In an era when megatalent agencies are the dominant force in Holly-wood, Casino is one of the last independents from the golden age of agenting. Many of today's so-called Young Turks could learn a lesson from the man who "Quinn Martin" dubbed "Candy" because of the sweet deals he got for his clients. The "Casino Stable of Stars" once included many show-biz giants, including: Jim "Mr. Magoo" Backus (1913–1989), Scatman Crothers (1910–1986), and currently Linda "I'm Still Here" Granger (birth date not available). I recently broke rye bread with the "Candy Man" at Nate and Al's delicatessen, where he revealed some of his innermost trade secrets.*

Flip When you finally retire and "hang up" your phone for good, how would you like to be remembered?

Candy Well, many of these mail-room clerks who parade around as agents today don't realize that I broke the television censorship barrier.

Flip Could you elaborate?

Candy I was the first agent to use the word "Fuck" in a contract negotiation with a major network. I don't think the kids today appreciate that.

Flip On behalf of all agents, I thank you. Do you remember your first client?

Candy Wilbur Throckmorton. You may remember him from the *Ed Sullivan Show*. He played the seal horns, he would move back and forth biting the little rubber bulbs. Great talent.

Flip Who are some of your current clients?

Candy Lately I've cut back my client roster so I can focus on some of my charity work and teach a course for the Learning Annex called "Screw unto Others, the Art of Agenting." But I still represent Linda Granger and a few others.

Flip What is the craziest thing you ever did to get a client work?

Candy Stalking.

Flip You stalked someone?

Candy No. I hired an actor to stalk one of my clients.

Flip Who?

Candy Linda Granger. I sent her on several castings one season. The first was for a TV pilot called "Rock-a-bye PI," about a rock star that moonlighted as a private investigator. The second was a kids' show called "Jeepers, Creepers the Turtle from Outer Space," but she got confused by the puppets. The third and most frustrating was for a movie of the week, "My Way, the Paul Anka Story." Linda was auditioning to play herself. She didn't get that part or any of the others.

Flip Is it hard for you to tell a client they didn't get a job?

Candy Just the ones with great asses, like Linda.

Flip How do you break it to them?

Candy I believe in never telling my clients the truth, but Linda is more than a client, she's a friend. So I told her that there was nothing out there for her unless she got some new publicity, like a tragedy or a scandal.

Flip How did she take it?

Candy Linda's a great gal, she offered to start drinking again. But we both agreed, "Been there, done that." Then it hit me, stalking. It was very hot that season. So I got on the horn and hired an actor to stalk her.

Flip You're a genius.

Candy The following morning the stalker arrived at Linda's house and she told him to follow her to the mall. Around noon she called me to say that the stalker was marvelous, everything was going great, and she was heading to the Valley to be threatened in front of Gelson's market. When I hung up I got a call from the actor I had hired, telling me he was sorry he had to cancel but that he had gotten a callback for "Disney on Ice."

Flip So who was following Linda?

Candy A real stalker, who chased her into a condemned, earthquake-damaged building and held her at knifepoint because of some psychosexual Linda Granger obsession.

Flip It must have been horrible for her.

Candy Yes and no. It had been a long time since a man had shown her that kind of attention. I think in a way she was touched. Plus, every TV station sent a news crew to cover it live. Linda was even on *Nightline*. My phones were ringing off the hook with offers for her.

Flip What happened to the stalker?

Candy The police shot him with a tranquilizer dart and arrested him. He just finished writing a movie of the week about the incident, with a possible part for Linda, and guess who's representing him?

Flip Candy Casino!

BEAUX MIRAGE CONDOS
RETIREMENT COMMUNITY

FERN ROSENTHAL ON FAME

People really don't know this, but I was once Miss Shaker Heights. Yeah, really! My girl-friends and I went down to the beach, and there was this beauty contest going on, and Linda Lundt dared me to enter. So I en-tered as a joke. I was really mak-ing fun of the whole thing. Before I knew it, we were down to three contestants, and I thought, "Fern, you don't want to be a runner-up all your life." (I was very motivated in those days.) *They asked us each a question, and mine was: "Would you like to be the first girl on the moon?" Right then and there I knew I had it. I said, "I don't need a fancy trip anywhere. I want to stay right here in Shaker Heights." When they put the crown on, I realized that the quickest way to become famous was to lie. Just look at that Pamela Lee, if she thinks anyone is fooled by those candy mountains, then I'm the Pope's wife!*

H.R.H. ON FAME

PIP

Bob Dylan, Your Highness.

H.R.H.

Oh. Do you know, I never understood a word you said. Never mind, here's the thing. We always have a problem finding a performer for the Christmas staff party at Windsor Castle. The Queen Mother's first choice was Neil Diamond, but he wanted to be picked up at the airport! The youngsters would like Oasis or Stone Temple Pilots, but one can't run the risk of having people who might urinate on the tapestries. No, you'd be perfect. You're moderately famous, and you're far too old to bother the chamber maids. There'll be no fee, or course, but you can expect a goose and a bottle of homemade cider. Good-bye.

COSMOtologist
the makeup magazine

May 14, 1997 — A Lazar World Publication — Volume 1, Issue 1

Sylvia
"Red" Lazar

The Craziest Thing I Ever Did!

Interview by
Sylvia "Red" Lazar

*R*uby Romaine is still one of Hollywood's top makeup artistes after fifty-two years in the business. In an age where blushes and bases are mixed by high-tech machinery with computer brains, Romaine prefers to do it the old-fashioned way, in a blender. She has done makeup for the great and the near

Ruby Romaine
Makeup Artiste

great. Bette Davis, Lana Turner, and Linda Granger are some of the faces she has painted. With over 720 movies and television shows to her credit, Romaine is the oldest living member of her union still working today. I recently sipped martinis with her at the Smog Cutter Lounge in Silverlake. While she has spent her life as a cosmetologist she claims the secret to preserving yourself can't be found in a compact or tube but only in a bottle. Here's looking at you, Ruby Romaine!

Red: How has Hollywood changed since you got started as a makeup artist?

Ruby: Well, it used to be a real elegant neighborhood, but now all the babies have earrings and you can smell the rice and beans in the air. It's turned into boom shakalacka-town.

Red: I was actually referring to the entertainment industry.

Ruby: Oh well, it's smuttier now than it was in the old days.

Red: How do you mean?

Ruby: Well, I never had to use a "beaver brush" when I worked for Mr. Minelli!

Red: What about behind the scenes?

Ruby: Listen dearie, I've been working on motion pictures since Noah was a sailor, and I know where all the bodies are buried. I know all the secrets.

Red: For instance?

Ruby: Well, do you know what Lana Turner, Tina Turner, and Ted Turner have in common?

Red: No, what?

Ruby: They've all been beaten by their spouses. I used to cover Lana's bruises from that Johnny Stompanato. If you ask me, the two of them were sickos. He knocked her around and she liked it. And poor little Cheryl just didn't understand. My daughter Desiree

was the same age. I know Desiree is a black name now, but back then it was a beautiful name. . . .

Red: Ruby, what's the craziest job you ever had?

Ruby: I guess that would be when I fixed up Miss Vivian Biltmore's kisser.

Red: Do you refer to your work on Miss Biltmore's Oscar-winning performance in *Faded Splendor*?

Ruby: Nope, this was last year. Her chauffeur, Klaus, came to my door saying my presence was requested at the Biltmore Estate. Well, I knew it wasn't an invitation to one of her swanky parties because she and I had a falling out forty years ago when she got me fired off a picture.

Red: Why did she do that?

Ruby: She accused me of being drunk. Which I was not. It was heat exhaustion, plain and simple. Besides, she had no right to talk, always nipping at the Dubonnet and popping those diet happy pills the studio gave her. . . .

Red: So did you go with her chauffeur?

Ruby: Yeah, I figured she needed me to give her a special glamour job for some lifetime achievement award—she was always getting those—"For services above and beyond the call of duty in the director's trailer" kinda thing. Anyhoo, when we got to her house, Vivian was taking a nap. She looked kinda pale, but nothing a lit-

tle rouge couldn't fix. So, I asked if we should wake her up so I could get to work. Then Mr. Fancy Pants says, "Madam Biltmore has taken her final repose."

Red: She was dead?

Ruby: As a dodo, Red.

Red: And he wanted you to make her up for the funeral?

Ruby: Bull's eye. At first I tell him, "You need a mortician not a beautician, honey." But he flashes a wad of cash at me and I figure a girl has got to eat.

Red: So you did her makeup?

Ruby: Yep! I even waxed her mustache, but when her upper lip came away on the cotton strip, I realized it was mold.

Red: How did it turn out?

Ruby: Pretty good. Klaus said I made her look beautiful, like the woman he once loved so long ago. Hell maybe they shouldn't have buried her.

Red: Making the dead look beautiful, now that's impressive.

Ruby: Red, it's like I always say, I'm not a star, I'm a star maker.

Ms. Hope Finch
P.O. Box 1749, Taconic Pkwy.
Connecticut
E-mail@www.lenslady.edu

"CAVIAR IS MURDER!"
SAVE THE UNBORN STURGEON,
FISH HAVE A RIGHT TO LIFE!

HOPE FINCH ON FAME

I'm taking a course in "Philosophy and How It Relates to Life Near the End of the Millennium." It's a great course, and Ms. Lattimer could teach in Utopia. The other day she went around the room and asked each of us: If we could have one famous person, living or dead, to dinner, who would it be? And I knew right away. It definitely would be Golda Meir . . . but I would invite Jesus over for dessert.

THE GYPSY CAB COMPANY

CHIC ON FAME

I get a lot of famous people in the cab. You know, I picked up Andrew Lloyd Webber once. He says to me, he want to make a musical of The Invisible Man. You know, no actors. I said, come on Andrew, you know, spend a few bucks. Do Phantom of the Opera. Now look, it's a big hit and what do I get? Not a note in the Playbill, not even a fucking Michael Crawford CD. That Faye Dunaway, you know, I warned her. I warned her about him.

TAXI

"EVERY DAY FRESH!!"

MRS. NOH NANG NING ON FAME

YEAH, YEAH, YEAH, I KNOW MANY FAMOUS PEOPLE. OH YEAH, THEY COME IN, THEY GIVE ME PICTURE, AND I PUT PICTURE ON WALL. I GOT MR. MARTY INGELS, MR. ARTIE JOHNSON. AND THIS ONE BIG, BIG STAR, AHHH . . . "TO MRS. NOHNANGNING, MY NUMBER-ONE FAN. YOURS ALWAYS, LINDA GRANGER." YEAH, SHE TAKE STUFF FROM ASS AND INJECT IT IN LIPS.

Alternative Lifestyles

FAME!

WITH ALL THE SAND TRAPPINGS

Interview by Felix "Flip" Lazar Jr.

Personality Profile

*C**hris Warner** sits across from me. She's pretty and looks very much like the aerobics treacher that she is (currently, however, she's taking a hiatus). Chris is the life companion to the professional golfer Midge Dexter, and their story, if you don't know, is subject to much public opinion. It started last year when they became notorious for their openly gay relationship. It was widely publicized when Midge won women's most prestigious golf title, the Slimline Classic.*

Q. So Chris, what was it that led you to "come out" in such a dramatic fashion?

A. Well, I guess it started the night before the final cut when we were watching TV. I happened to see Lee Janzen winning a golf tournament. His wife ran onto the green and practically leaped into his arms. It made me sad because I knew I couldn't do that when Midge won a tournament. It was hard for me, keeping everything a secret, telling everyone I was her nutritionist. I just didn't get why it had to be like that, I mean all our friends—Sue and Robin, Jill and Wendy—they didn't try to fool anyone. Also, that day I'd heard our friends Kim and Roberta were having a baby with their cable guy, and I felt really envious. When I told Midge she got really mad and said, "That's great, but they're not in the public eye like me!"

Q. So, in your own words, what happened the next day at the Slimline Classic?

A. Well, when Midge sunk that final putt I was so proud. All I wanted to do was go and be with her, but I knew I couldn't. Just as I was preparing to go to the clubhouse for a private locker room celebration, I heard Midge shout out, "C'mon, baby. C'mon down!" I looked at her standing on the course with her arms wide open and I knew she meant it. All the years of guilt and repression lifted from me as I ran through the crowd, onto the green, and into her arms. As we kissed, the flashes were going off around us like firecrackers. It was very emotional. Finally after all that time, to be able to show our feelings to the world . . . literally. It was great. It was the start of that famous '97 Coming Out season: first us, then Ellen DeGeneres and Anne Heche; and Melissa Etheridge and Julie Cypher had their baby that year, too.

Q. Being a Christian, how do you feel about your relationship with Midge?

A. What we feel and who we are isn't wrong. And the real God knows that!

Q. Since Midge must spend a lot of her day on the golf course, how do you spend most of your time?

A. I've been thinking of starting a line of motivational golf club covers that say "Keep it in the short grass" and stuff like that. I was always good at needlepoint and I like to crochet, so I made this one for Midge [she picks up a club cover and puts it on her hand like a puppet]. *"Hi, I'm Charlie Chipmunk— and I'm gonna keep your three-wood all nice and warm."*

Q. How did your lifestyle change with your sudden notoriety?

A. Not that much really. The people at the Dental Dam Female Condom Company offered us a million dollars to promote their product. But in the end we didn't think it would help Midge's image as a serious golfer. She did do a spread for the milk campaign, but that was tough for her because she's lactose intolerant. We also led a march for the American Lesbian League, there were T-shirts made up with us on them, and it was really weird to see our faces plastered over thousands of strangers' boobs!

Q. So it sounds as if things are going great and you're happy?

A. Very. Sometimes, Midge says that she doesn't deserve me, but I think I'm the lucky one! I mean I never thought I'd be famous. I thank the Lord every day that she took me out of that crummy diner in Barstow. I remember it clearly. I asked her if she wanted to know what the special was, and she said, "Baby, I'm hopin' it's you." Isn't that romantic?

VAN NUYS SAVINGS & LOAN

KAY CLARK
ASSISTANT BRANCH MANAGER

KAY CLARK ON FAME

Thanks to my position as foreign teller at the Van Nuys Savings & Loan I had occasion to meet Pablo Escobar, the notorious Colombian drug lord, multiple murderer, and fugitive from justice. You see, they thought he was hiding in the untamed jungles of darkest Peru, when in point of fact, he was living above a donut shop in Studio City, and he came into my branch to cash a check. Well I hesitated when I heard the name, and then for some reason, I don't know, call it a whim, I cashed the check. I still don't know why. And then he held my hand and said, "You're a good woman. If you ever want anybody killed, you know where to come to." Anyway I never did anything about it because he didn't leave a business card. Which is probably why Mother's still alive today. Mustn't say that. Mustn't, mustn't say it.

A LARK WITH KAY CLARK

"WORK CAN BE LIKE A RODEO... YOU PUT UP WITH A LOT OF BULL, AND THERE'S ALWAYS SOME CLOWN WANTING YOUR ATTENTION!"

"I'LL TUMBLE FOR YA!"

RAYLEEN GIBSON
Professional Stuntwoman &
Chief Executive Officer of AAAH
(Aged Animal Actor's Home)

RAYLEEN GIBSON ON FAME

I do a lot of stunts for famous people! Here I am about to fall down a flight of thirty-two stairs with no padding except in my brassiere because I'm supposed to look like the star, and she's got humungous, gigantic jugs. If you want to know the truth, she wore a couple of these pads herself, but hers were internal, if you know what I mean! But I suppose it's all a part of show business, you always have to look good. Take this falling down stairs, I suppose you could say it's a specialty of mine. But there's a knack to it. As a professional stuntwoman, I have to fall bing-bang-boom while keeping my legs together. You know you got to be careful about that, you don't wanna ruin the shot with your crotch wide open. You know, shoot a big beaver and you're gonna have to do the whole shot over again!

CHAPTER
NINE
MOVIES

TRACEY ULLMAN ON MOVIES

Going to the movies in England when I was a child was not a pleasant experience. Living in the sticks, as I did, our local cinema was a nasty '60s-style concrete box, showing scratchy prints of American movies, many months after their original release. Having spent a couple of hours trying to park your car, you were greeted by a surly woman in a lemon and lime uniform who seemed to run the whole place single-handedly. She tore the tickets, pointed you to your seat with a flashlight, sold you stale "American-style" popcorn, and on one occasion threw out a group of teenage boys who had a farting competition during a showing of *Rollerball.*

So my ambition for many years was to go to the cinema in the West End of London, where the Queen went once a year to see a film that was deemed suitable for royal viewing, like *Towering Inferno* or *The Way We Were.*

At age fourteen I finally got my wish. It was a boring day in school and my friend Leslie Ash and I sneaked out. We headed for Leicester Square to see the film version of *Once Is Not Enough,* Jacqueline Susann's sexy novel. The foyer was wonderful, thick red carpets, gilt and brass everywhere, and a specially imported machine that made fresh "American-style" popcorn. It was just the two of us in the audience that day, apart from the obligatory dirty old man in a raincoat, who sat right next to us despite there being over a thousand vacant seats.

The film was terrible, but terrible in a very watchable sort of way, rather like *Showgirls* or my personal favourite, *Lonely Lady* with Pia Zadora. We were transfixed until a huge rat ran from the side of the stage, under the seats, and scrabbled across our feet. Our screams brought the manager and made Mr. Pac-O-Mac run out of a side exit. The manager chose not to believe us and made us very nervous by asking why we weren't at school, our rolled up grey skirts and school ties tied bandanna-style round our heads being a dead giveaway. So we didn't stay for the rest of the film, and to this day I have not seen the end of *Once Is Not Enough* but it's no great loss, I like to call it "Two-thirds Was Quite Sufficient."

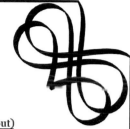

Trevor Ayliss
& Barrington LeTissier
Willows Mews Cottage
Osterly on the Green
Middlesex, MD12 6HE
(Come off the M40 at the Robin Hood Roundabout)

TREVOR AYLISS ON MOVIES

I do cry at romantic films. I can't help it, I have a very low tear threshold. But I've never cried at *Gone With the Wind*. Straight people find it the biggest weepy of all, but when I see that Rhett Butler with his Village People mustache and his tight-riding britches walking out on that squeaky girl, I know he's doing exactly the right thing. And I know where he's going, too—right into the arms of that dusty cavalry lieutenant we saw in reel one. And then, the two of them elope to San Francisco, where they become the first blacksmith and leather worker who won't do horses. Perfect.

MOVIE POLL

American Cinema's
Hollywood Monsterplex

Name: *Ruby Romaine*
Address: *Hollywood*
Occupation: *Makeup artist*
Age: *72.* ←———————

*If you don't believe me,
I'll chop off my arm
and you can count the rings!*

Ethnic Background: *White (last one in this neighborhood!)*
Income: *None of your Beeswax!*
Name of Movie: *Satan's Playground.*
Theater Number: *33*

How would you rate the convenience and design of the Monsterplex?
*Piss-poor! I had to take two escalators and a people mover to get to
the lower concourse concession stand, which was closed! There wasn't
a soul to ask where to catch the tram to the toilet, although it would
probably have been quicker to go to Long Beach!*

Any suggestions to improve our concession stand?
*How about selling a map to the theater, or maybe something a normal
human being would eat, like Milk Duds and Hershey bars instead of
yogurt pretzels and all-natural kiwi-tangerine soda.*

How did you find the decor of the Monsterplex?
*Like a neon whorehouse! Whatever happened to movie theaters with
red velvet curtains, chandeliers, balconies, real butter on the popcorn,
and real movie stars on the screen?*

Did you find your seat(s) comfortable?

The movie didn't keep me in my seat but the yum on it sure did! And by the way, those little cup holders you got are worthless. I ordered the Bladder Kill size 7-Up which didn't fit because it was too <u>big</u>, and my little flask of medication smashed on the floor because it was too <u>small.</u>

Did you find the staff to be courteous?

Everybody told me to enjoy the movie about fifteen times like androids. But when I tried to have a little cocktail and a smoke, Pedro the usher came bouncing down the aisle like a little jumping bean and started babbling on about how Monsterplex is a family theater and doesn't allow cigarettes or liquor. Then why the hell were you showing a movie about the devil with a bunch of buck-naked teachers on a merry-go-round for!?! Tell me I was asleep and I was just dreaming I was on the planet of the assholes. When I asked for my money back he told me all I could get was a coupon for readmission. I'd rather be readmitted to Sing-Sing!

How did you enjoy your overall moviegoing experience?

About as much as I enjoyed my hysterectomy!

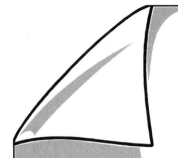

Wimpman, KROSS, and Wussman
"You name it, we'll sue it." *(Since 1987)*
PENTHOUSE
F. LEE BAILEY LEGAL CENTER
100 CANON DRIVE
BEVERLY HILLS

FROM THE COMMAND STATION OF SYDNEY KROSS

I know eventually they'll make a movie of my life. What I think about a lot is who is going to play me. It can't be Sandra Bullock because she has that weird straight hair. Elisabeth Shue isn't pretty enough. And Anna Nicole Smith ... well, why don't you just shoot me in the heart?

VAN NUYS SAVINGS & LOAN

KAY CLARK
ASSISTANT BRANCH MANAGER

KAY CLARK ON MOVIES

I'll never forget the first time I went to the cinema on my own. Just me, unaccompanied. Buying my own ticket and my own ice cream and settling down in the front row of the old Muswell Hill Odeon. And when the lights dimmed, there was this tremendous feeling of excitement and anticipation. I'm told sex is something like that.

Just as the credits came up they flashed this scratchy writing on the screen—"Will Kay Clark go home at once." And I did, running all the way, to find out that my mother had had one of her funny turns. She had her last turn on Tuesday, just as I was halfway through <u>Rumble in the Bronx.</u> 'Course I watch them on video now. So I only have to pop into the bedroom.

A LARK WITH KAY CLARK

WHEN AT WORK, NEVER LOSE SIGHT OF WHAT'S IMPORTANT... LUNCH!

H.R.H. ON MOVIES

PIP

Ms. Demi Moore, Your Highness.

H.R.H.

Oh yes. If my memory serves me correctly, you were the person who posed nude and pregnant on the cover of *Vanity Fair*. It must take a certain kind of courage to do anything that vulgar. But this is rather fortuitous. I was wondering what to buy the Royal children for Christmas, and then I thought they might like those caps from that ghastly Planet Hollywood where, I believe, your husband works as a waiter. I'm sure you can arrange a discount, which one would appreciate. Why don't you have a word with my Private Secretary and he'll give you their hat sizes. Good-bye.

BEAUX MIRAGE CONDOS
RETIREMENT COMMUNITY

FERN ROSENTHAL ON MOVIES

When I was dating, I loved to go to the movies. But once in a while some of the boys tried to get fresh. They had this trick where they would buy a box of popcorn, cut a hole in the bottom, and stick their thingy in there. Then they asked if you wanted a handful of popcorn. But when you reached in you got a handful of schmeckle. I was wise to this. So when Howard Lefkowitz tried to pull this on me, I reached in, grabbed him by his putz, dragged him up the aisle, out into the lobby, and dumped him there. Then I went back into the theater to see the rest of the movie. It was called *Love Is a Many Splendored Thing;* I adore that picture. But then I'm a hopeless romantic.

Ms. Hope Finch
P.O. Box 1749, Taconic Pkwy.
Connecticut
E-mail@www.lenslady.edu

Pop Quizzes Not Pills

PRO-EDUCATION/ANTI-DRUGS

HOPE FINCH ON MOVIES

Last week, I went to the Student Union to see <u>Fantasia</u> with my roommate Crosby and her friend Chloe. I was really blown away by it. I thought that Walt Disney made the movie to try to warn people against destroying the planet and desecrating our natural resources with pollution. And that we should rise above animal instinct and live in harmony with each other. But they said they thought it was just about some hippopotamuses in tutus, dancing to boring classical music.

Today our Film History teacher, Mr. Capewell, said that Disney had a strict policy of no social commentary and that he made the movie as pure entertainment.

I don't know why I imagined all that, especially since Crosby and Chloe were the ones who took two Herbal Ecstasy pills with a bottle of tequila before the movie, and all I had was a frozen yogurt.

THE GYPSY CAB COMPANY

CHIC ON MOVIES

The other day I go to the video store and I rent a movie called <u>S.O.B.</u> and in this movie, I see the tits of Mary Poppins. Not that I haven't seen them before — I had her in my cab once, and, well, I'm Chic. But on the big screen, even better.

VIRGINIA BUGGE ON MOVIES

Excerpts from Virginia Bugge's Diary

Sunday, June 2nd

Tomorrow the American film crew arrives at 5 A.M. Timmy seems to be getting cold feet about giving them the run of Bugge Manor. He mumbled something about men in muddy boots trampling all over the begonias. But I told him in no uncertain terms that we are letting them film <u>A King's Ransom</u> here because that's exactly what we're going to charge them. The five thousand pounds a week they're paying us will take care of Simon's school fees and the villa near Siena this summer!

Monday, June 3rd

Day 1. The film crew arrived this morning. The very tanned director Bud wandered into the kitchen and told Timmy what a marvellous home we had and what a wonderful location it was going to be. And then Timmy said something jolly spiteful, "Actually it's eighteenth century, about seventy years later than the period in which your film is set." I could have killed him. But Bud very graciously said that he doubted if the average American teenager in a Midwest multiplex gave a shit, and then he went back to his trailer. "And I don't suppose they care if Charles the First sounds like

Meeting Bud the Director

Barney Rubble from the _Flintstones!_" Timmy shouted after him. Thankfully, I don't think he heard, and I shut Timmy up by giving him a sharp smack across the patella with a meat tenderizer.

~~Thursday, June 6th~~

All's going well, Bud has found me indispensable as a continuity advisor and calls me his head girl. This afternoon we were filming in the main hall. It was a pivotal scene in which Lord Percy slaps Sir Richard in the face with his glove and says, "A duel, sir, at dawn." To which Sir Richard retorts, "Then we shall see how pink is the colour of your Royalist blood!" It was a terribly dramatic moment, until Timmy barged in through the front door (Parliament had let out early). Bud screamed, "Cut! Who let that a—hole in here!" to which the assistant director replied, "She a—hole owns the house." I've never been so humiliated in my life.

Friday 7th

Today Timmy was confined to quarters. I locked him in the attic, where he seemed perfectly happy with a large jug of lemon barley water and a wireless so he could listen to the cricket match. In the afternoon Rob Trasker, the star of the picture, asked me if I wouldn't mind helping him with his English accent. I told him that he had to hit the 't' in gentleman a bit harder. And I reminded him that "it's all

Timmy takes a terrible Polaroid

to do with where you put your tongue." "I'll pretend I didn't hear that . . . you brrrrazen hussy!" he replied. I turned bright red and then he gallantly kissed my hand. I do believe he was flirting with me. If only I'd had a chance to work on Kevin Costner's accent, I could have saved _Prince of Thieves_.

The makeup girl took this Polaroid of Rob and me.

P.S. I've noticed something quite peculiar about Bud, even though he's been in England for two months now, and it's been a frightful summer, he's still gloriously tanned!?!

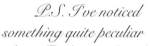 Saturday 8th

When I let Timmy out of the attic this morning, he was in a very bad temper; "I saw you with that Trasker, giggling in the garden like a prepubescent schoolgirl." I simply explained that I was giving him elocution lessons. He told me it was a bloody waste of time because "People from California only have twelve words in their vocabulary, two of which are _surf board_!" Well it's true I find these film people amusing and glamourous, unlike Timmy's fat Cabinet friends, whose farts and belches are more riveting than their conversation.

P.S. I found out how Bud has managed to stay so tanned! He's commandeered the sun bed from Pamela Smythe's solarium and put it in his hotel room! Last night he overloaded everything, what with his Stair-Master, fax machine, and satellite dish, and blacked out the whole village.

Wednesday 12th

Today was the last day of the shoot. The crew packed everything up and all they left behind were some holes in the lawn where the catering tent had been. Rob thanked me for our hospitality, gave me a King's Ransom jacket and cap, and told me that he would see us at the premiere. Of course, I knew we wouldn't attend; getting Timmy to the pictures is rather "mission impossible." I reached out to shake his hand, but he took me in his arms and gave me a rather passionate kiss. I felt a frisson of excitement, similar to the feeling I get when driving over the cattle grid in the Range Rover. I shall miss him. I shall miss them all. But I suppose that I do have plenty to keep me busy — the village fête next week, those gooseberries to bottle for the winter — all sorts of things going on all over the place, really. . . .

Addendum

It's 2 A.M. I'm writing this now so that I don't forget exactly how it happened. Timmy was a little later than usual coming up to the bedroom, I had thought he was still brooding. I'd just gotten under the covers when all of a sudden he burst in, dressed from head to toe like a cavalier, dangerously waving around a sword (that he'd pilfered from the prop truck), "I have come to take you by devious routes to the brink of desire, and beyond," he challenged. "I will brook no objections nor delays, for my passion is burgeoning and I have a long-felt want. So, my wanton wench, my coquette, my shameless . . . pom-pom girl of the night. Look upon Jeremy Pinkstaff and swoon away!" And with that he dropped his britches! What could I say, except . . . "Action!"

FAVORITE

Virginia Bugge—*Equus.*

Janie Pillsworth —Any Peter Greenaway, or at a pinch, Wim Wenders

Ruby Romaine — *The Lost Weekend.* (I helped Ray Milland research his role, and it took more than a weekend, I can tell ya!)

Chic – *Taxi Driver.* Isn't that fucking obvious, my friend!?!

Fern Rosenthal —Any of Barbra's. I loved *The Mirror Has Two Faces—and Four Chins* (her lighting guy's a schmuck!)

Hope Finch —Spalding Gray's *Swimming to Cambodia* (some philistine had placed this in the sports section at my local Block-buster!)

FILMS

Linda Granger – *The Venetian Caper* (1972). Starring myself and Tony Franciosa—it contains surely the most exciting gondola chase sequence ever shot—which finishes with yours truly in the drink! (Thank God for waterproof mascara!)

Rayleen Gibson—*Hook!* Crap movie—***GREAT*** stunts.

Erin McColl —It was this film of a concert . . . and the screen was like split into eight or ten boxes . . . and it was in this field and there was a lotta mud and porta cabins . . . and there were all these cool bands and . . . hey, I think I was in it! Fuck, what was it called?

MRS. NOH NANG NING—*Escape from L. A.* They film all decaying desolate armageddon scenes on my street. Craft/Service man buy all my donuts first thing in morning. I play Paigow all afternoon!

CHAPTER
TEN
HEALTH

TRACEY ULLMAN ON HEALTH

I have always been a Western medicine kind of girl. Brought up in England in the '60s with a Nationalised Health Service in full swing. It was the pill-popping generation, and it was all free! If you went to the doctor and he didn't give you three or four different medications, you were disappointed. Especially after having sat in a crowded waiting room with thirty other sniffling Brits, fed on a diet of steak and kidney puddings, overcooked vegetables, and endless cups of tea.

And no one thought of working out! A Sunday afternoon walk to aid the digestion of lunch was acceptable. . . . We would go to places like Box Hill in Dorking, get out of the car, walk 20 feet and, shielding our lighters from the wind, puff on cigarettes and check our watches, waiting for the pubs to open. Sometimes when we were sitting outside, drinking lagers and lime on a summer's evening, we would see the extraordinary sight of a long-distance runner go by. How we laughed and taunted people like that, "Go on mate, you might catch the others!" We would shout, "Who wears short shorts!"

I hated sports at school; we had to wear aertex shirts and navy blue knickers. I remember a vast expanse of pink and white mottled thighs jiggling around as the girls netball team practiced in the frosty playground. We had swimming once a week in the indoor pool, which was a 30 percent water 70 percent chlorine mix. Just standing by the pool having your feet checked for fungus made you weep buckets, and for the rest of the day the class had eyes like albino rabbits.

I started to dance at the age of twelve when I went to stage school, but it didn't stop me from smoking forty cigarettes a day by the time I was sixteen. All dancers smoked, drank, ate nothing, and wore 4-inch platform shoes—our bodies were indestructible!

Then when I was twenty-one, I was working on a television play in Manchester with an idol of mine, the actress Julie Walters. I had a small role as her sister, and I came up from London and stayed in an enormous old Railway Hotel, a monument to Victorian architecture. The first night Julie asked me to have a drink in the bar; I was thrilled, and matched her Guinness for Guinness, followed by numerous glasses of full-bodied red wine. It was a great night and I went to bed at 1 A.M. knowing I had a 5:30 wake-up call. When the alarm went off, up I jumped up and stepped into my cavernous marble bathroom. As I was running the taps I carelessly spun open my Yves St. Laurent bubble bath and lost control of the chunky metal cap, which flew out of my hand and hit the floor — the noise was deafening! I groggily chased it around and around, hoping to smother it with a towel, but I lost my balance and tripped over the bidet. I sat on the floor holding my throbbing head and burst into tears. I tried to take some aspirin but I couldn't look at anything that white. I don't know how I got through the day, and I got no sympathy from Julie, who was full of the joys of spring, of course.

This was my first and last hangover, and this sobering incident set me on the path to the aerobicised, organic, vegetarian, homeopathic, boring world I live in today.

KAY CLARK ON HEALTH

Get sick? Me? I'm never poorly. I have been working at the Van Nuys Savings & Loan for fifteen years and have never missed a day through illness. At the first sign of any malady, I rub a half a jar of menthol embrocation on my chest. I wrap my upper extremities in a poultice soaked in bay rum and mustard powder. I take four tablespoons of castor oil, and four of liquid paraffin for good measure. I do believe the cure is far worse than the disease. "Stop malingering, Kay," says Mother. "Nobody else has earned the right to be sick around here." Mother's marvellous, she really is.

A LARK WITH KAY CLARK

"IMPORTANT NOTICE FROM UPPER MANAGEMENT. WE CAN SO FIND OUR BUTTS WITH BOTH HANDS!"

Bugge Manor (Since 1578)

Virginia Bugge
& Timothy Bugge
(M.P. for Greater Diddlesbury)
Bugge Manor
Wrencham Hollow
Diddlesbury

VIRGINIA BUGGE ON HEALTH

There's no such thing as a British diet. The working classes eat tinned peas and far too many sweets. The middle class like pasta and frozen desserts from Harrods. The upper class always prefer things that are baked, caught, or shot that afternoon. They also love eggs, marmalade, masses of red meat, clotted cream, anchovies, marzipan, and mustard. Except Timmy's brother. He lives entirely off Hunza apricots and doesn't wear socks. He fell out of a tree house when he was very young and has always been slightly odd.

Ms. Hope Finch
P.O. Box 1749, Taconic Pkwy.
Connecticut
E-mail@www.lenslady.edu

O.D.D. (Official Designated Driver)
Certified to Chauffeur People with the
Following Addictions:
Alcohol:
Marijuana:
Cocaine:
Heroin:

HOPE FINCH ON HEALTH

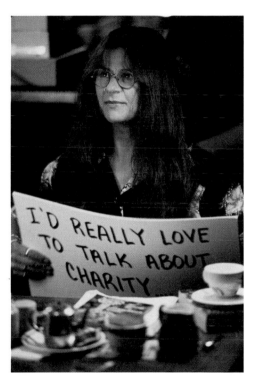

Normally I'm really peppy. I'm on the swim team and I play volleyball. Then last week I got this energy drip thing and I'm like I just wanna lie on my bed and watch AMC.

My friend Clyde, who's in Pre-Med, thinks maybe I got bitten by a parakeet when I was a kid and got infected with this deadly virus from the Amazon, or one of those places. And if the microorganisms are harmful then it would weaken my immune system and cause tissue degeneration and incapacitate the reproductive process of my red corpuscles so that I might have to be quarantined and live in a plastic bubble....

Or I could just have a cold.

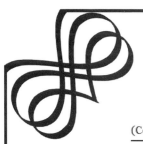

Trevor Ayliss
& Barrington LeTissier
Willows Mews Cottage
Osterly on the Green
Middlesex, MD12 6HE

(Come off the M40 at the Robin Hood Roundabout)

TREVOR AYLISS ON HEALTH

I used to go out with a neurosurgeon, and I tell you, while I was with him, I've never been such a nervous wreck in all my life. You see, he used to sleepwalk, and sometimes I'd wake in the early

hours of the morning to find him scrubbing up in the bathroom. One night, I opened my eyes and he was standing over me, fast asleep, holding an electric toothbrush. God knows what he was going to do with it, but he looked frighteningly confident. Anyway, we struggled on for about six months, then I told him I couldn't take the anxiety, and in a fit of pique, he went off with an anesthesiologist. I figure at least now he's probably getting some sleep.

The Motion Picture Fund Health Clinic
Dolly Parton Mammography Center

Patient Information Form

Name: *Ruby Romaine*

Address: *264 1/2 Fernando Valenzuela Blvd. Hollywood, CA 90036*
(formerly Appleby Street when the neighborhood was still part of America!)

Phone Number: *Temporarily disconnected*

Occupation: *Makeup Artiste*

Insurance Company: *Motion Picture & Television Fund*

Are you allergic to anything? *Vitamins and mineral water*

Do you drink alcohol? *Only to sterilize my intestines and kill mouth bacteria. It works.*

Do you smoke? *NO! Those coffin nails are terrible for you.*

Breast size: *38 Double "D"*

Reason for your visit: *I've been getting my insurance through the Makeup Artist Guild for 42 years. Now all of a sudden they have a new policy and they tell me I've got to get a checkup or they'll drop me like a hot potato. So let's make sure I pass this exam or you'll lose two of your biggest customers.*

When was the last time you had this procedure done?

It's been several years. I had to go clear down
to San Diego because my bazoombas were too big
for the old Mammarygram gizmo you had here.
Thank god Miss Dolly Parton donated this new one!

Additional comments: Lighten up on the pressure.
Last time it felt like they had my tit in a vise.
I hadn't been squeezed that hard since I worked
with Anthony Quinn.

Checkup results:

Miss Romaine's mammogram revealed general good conditon of the breasts.

Abnormalities:

Romaine (age 72) began to lactate under the pressure of the scanner plates

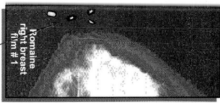

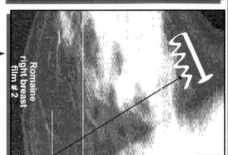

Romaine right breast film # 1

Romaine right breast film # 2

Miss Romaine's breasts were so enormous that two films were necessary for each, even on the Macro-dyne Super plus XXL536.

A metallic object that appears to be a bobby pin. Miss Romaine believes that she sat on it 43 years ago while working on the film *Mogambo*.

Notes:

Miss Romaine was warned about the hazards of cigarettes after Dr. Aswan detected what appeared to be a yellow nicotine stain on her index finger. She denied yet again that she smokes and claimed that the stain was "Baby Blonde" hair dye from a root job she once gave to Barbara Eden.

Recommendations:

Radiologist Dr. Aswan feels that Miss Romaine no longer needs to receive yearly testing. Patient concurs and said, "Even if I get a lump way out on the tip of the Matterhorn, by the time it got to base camp, I'd be 105."

"EVERY DAY FRESH!!!"

MRS. NOH NANG NING ON HEALTH

EVERY DAY I FACE MY DRAGON – BRING HIM THROUGH BODY – TO RELEASE THROUGH CHAKRA ON CROWN. THEN YOU EMBRACE TIGER – COMBINING EARTH AND HEAVEN IN YOUR DEN TIER. THIS RELEASE WATERFALL OF TENSION – AWAKEN BOWEL – AND LOWER CHOLESTEROL – BRING PEEAACE. THEN I EAT FOUR DONUT AND GO TO WORK. . . .

MANHATTAN REVIEW MAGAZINE

from the editor's desk..

JANIE PILLSWORTH ON HEALTH

When my son took ill, I brought him to my acupuncturist, Mr. Wang Ping, but the needles made him cry. So I brought him to the herbalist, Baba Ram Bada, but the elixirs made him nauseous. Next, we did breathing exercises with my yoga master, Sri Miranda G, but my son couldn't sustain his prana. Then my mother got a hold of him. She put him to bed, read him storybooks, gave him hot tea with lemon, and he got better . . . but how banal!

HEALTHY, WEALTHY & WEISSMAN
by Bella Weissman

"Race for Your Life"

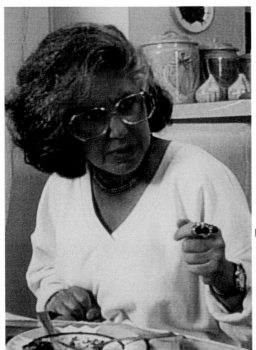

Jobie Wolff

The first annual "Boca Raton Marathon" in the Galleria Mall was won by the Beau Mirage Condo's very own Jobie Wolff. It was a grueling 25 laps around the mall, including the alcove near J.C. Penney. Seniors from all around South Florida competed for the top prize of a $2,000.00 dream shopping spree at SupeRX Drugs. The Florida Association of Condo Dwellers recommends walking as the best exercise and the mall as the healthiest place to do it. Many seniors can't breathe the fresh air in South Florida because of

An Apple a Day
by
Sylvia Wienrib

Did you know that eating before you go to bed causes indigestion? Have dinner at 4:30 P.M. and save the heartache.

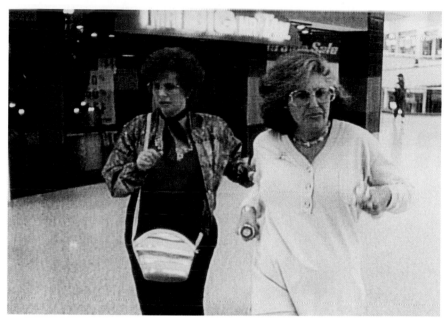

allergies. While dates are a good source of fiber which keeps you regular, the date palm is notorious for its nose-clogging pollen. Therefore, many seniors prefer mall-walking in a climate-controlled air-filtered environment. Another Beau Mirage resident who attended the marathon as a spectator was Fern Rosenthal. "Malls are for shopping and Richard Simmons is for exercise," says Rosenthal. "All that walking in circles makes me feel like a hamster, I'd rather sweat to the oldies."

Get well wishes go out to Herman Spitlick, who slipped and broke his hip during the eighteenth lap of the mall walk. Mrs. Spitlick reports, "We're suing, who mops floors at 6:00 in the morning?"

Overheard at the Health Spa

A certain redhead with the initials F.R. was heard to say the following: "There's been a lot of publicity about the conflict between Blacks and Jews. But whenever Michael Jackson gets sick, he goes straight to Cedars-Sinai Hospital!"

Mondo Condo
Beau Mirage News and Views

 ## A MESSAGE FROM CONDO PRESIDENT JOBIE WOLFF

Christie, our Aquacise instructor, has complained that several men in her class have not been wearing the proper undergarments with their swim trunks. And furthermore that one male student in particular has exposed himself to her, shouting, "Look at me, I'm Free Willy!" Please cease and desist, or your pool tags will be revoked.

Also we have recently had our Liability Insurance cut back. It will no longer cover skin cancer. Therefore, during the hours of 11:00 A.M. to 3:30 P.M. no one will be allowed in the pool area in bathing suits. During those hours you must wear a shirt and slacks to the pool, as well as sunblock factor 75!

Finally some good news. Emergency panic buttons have been installed in the laundry rooms. You will no longer be required to do your wash with your "Designated Buddy," but it is still recommended.

Remember, stay alert and stay alive!

THE GYPSY CAB COMPANY

CHIC ON HEALTH

I see these guys in the gym working out, with the tight Rocky Mountain pants. If you want my opinion, why spend all that energy pumping iron when you could be pumping girls? I have the body of a thirty-five year old, but I have the dick of a teenager. It wakes me up in the morning, it points out the best chicks, sometimes it even drives the cab. You should see it make a U-turn.

CHAPTER
ELEVEN
POLITICS

TRACEY ULLMAN ON POLITICS

I am not a political animal, and I shy away from having my celebrity used for political events. I feel unless you really know something about the issue, shut up! But once I was in New York at a photo session for a movie magazine, and I got a call from the legendary theatre director Joe Papp, telling me that he was ten blocks away in a notorious slum district where squatters were about to be evicted by the city. "Please come down!" Joe said. "We have the media alerted, and there'll be much more interest if you're here!"

Now I adored Joe Papp and was very much hoping he would give me a job in that summer's Shakespeare in the Park production, so I told the photographer I was popping out for ten minutes and ran down to my limousine, beautifully made up, dressed in a fabulous Jean-Paul Gaultier suit. The driver seemed somewhat surprised by my destination request and had to drop me a block away due to the police cars and news vans. I pushed through the crowd until I found Joe. He was delighted to see me and quickly gave me the task of working a pulley that was sending up food supplies to the threatened inhabitants. The great unwashed looked out of the window above and cheered me on, holding up snotty nosed infants to see their comrade. "Look!" shouted Joe to the media. "Tracey Ullman is with us! She knows that the eviction of these needy victims is a disgrace and can only profit the greedy capitalist land barons who are devoid of human compassion!" More cheers greeted this declaration, and I pulled for all I was worth, even though I had broken two nails and had rope burns on my delicate palms. But I wanted Joe to see that I could take direction, and by now I was very much into my character of an American revolutionary.

Unfortunately my silent role was not going to suffice, and Joe relieved me of my task and brought me forward to be interviewed. "What do you hope to achieve here today?" asked one. "What would you like to tell the mayor?" said another. "You're not a citizen of this country," a particularly belligerent man said. "What you're doing is illegal, you're going to be arrested!" Now I was scared, I was still waiting for my green card, and I had to be back at the photo session, they'd ordered Maine lobster for my lunch!!!

I was desperate to get out of there, I could hear myself making awkward statements like "Homelessness is a universal problem, we have it in England too!" I longed for someone to ask me about my next project, my favourite recipe, how my daughter Mabel was behaving, so I could return to the comfortable world of comedy.

Suddenly I saw my limo driver beckoning me from a side street. I kissed Joe on both cheeks and made my exit. I waved once more to my brothers and made a mental note to send them *Tracey Ullman Show* T-shirts; on second thought, sweatshirts would probably be warmer, and then I ran. Well, all's well that ends well, and my audition was successful, I got the part of Kate opposite Morgan Freeman as Petruchio that summer in a glorious production of *Taming of the Shrew*.

Bugge Manor (Since 1578)

Virginia Bugge
& Timothy Bugge
(M.P. for Greater Diddlesbury)
Bugge Manor
Wrencham Hollow
Diddlesbury

VIRGINIA BUGGE ON POLITICS

It's been a long time since England's had an effective prime minister. The last man fit for the job was Margaret Thatcher.

"EVERY DAY FRESH!!!"

MRS. NOH NANG NING ON POLITICS

IN MY COUNTRY, YOU VOTE HOW THEY TELL YOU, OR YOU GET BATON IN KIDNEY!

H.R.H. ON POLITICS

PIP

President Clinton, Your Highness.

H.R.H.

I've met several of your predecessors over the years. The Reagans were perfectly affable, though they were always holding hands, which one finds dubious at their age. Nixon was a man who never looked comfortable, rather like someone who's taken a suppository and is waiting for it to work. And when I was younger I sat next to President Kennedy at a state dinner. While they were serving sorbet, he talked of the special relationship between our two great nations and put his hand up my skirt, for which he received a dessert fork in the testicles.

Why don't you play us a tune on your saxophone after dinner and spare us one of your hour-long speeches? I'm sure we'll all be immensely grateful. Good-bye.

Wimpman, KROSS, and Wussman
"You name it, we'll sue it." *(Since 1987)*
PENTHOUSE
F. LEE BAILEY LEGAL CENTER
100 CANON DRIVE
BEVERLY HILLS

FROM THE COMMAND STATION OF SYDNEY KROSS

SYDNEY KROSS ON POLITICS

I love politicians, they give us lawyers someone to look down on!

The Tara Estates

A Gated & Graceful Community

Birdie Godsen

BIRDIE GODSEN ON POLITICS

My daughter and I are going to a meeting of the "We Hate Hillary Club." A bunch of us girls all get together once a month at the Marriott Dining Room over in Greenville. Tonight's topic is: "Hillary Rodham Clinton: Why Three Names Are One Too Many." Sissy's coming with me today because she's starting her own club with a bunch of her little girlfriends. It's called the "We Hate Chelsea Club." Isn't that great? It's something we like to do as a family.

THE GYPSY CAB COMPANY

CHIC ON POLITICS

American politics are all fucked up. Everybody freaks out each time a politician's caught with a girlie showing off his Washington Monument. Listen, my friend, I like a public official who gets laid. The leaders of our country have to think. And no one can think without having sex four, five times a day.

TAXI

RUBY ROMAINE ON POLITICS

When my son Buddy was seven, they chose him from over a hundred other youngsters to be the Tasty Bread boy on TV. You remember — he was famous. Everywhere he went, kids mobbed him. Then, when he was about seventeen, he was watching TV and he turned to me and said, "Mom, I wanta be in that." It was the Vietnam War, and, well, he came back home with a lot of problems. Before Buddy moved back here with me, he was living in Washington, right across from the White House. Had a little corrugated home he set up there. See, lotta folks make that leap from show-biz to politics — Ronald Reagan, Sonny Bono, Gopher from the _Loveboat_ . . .

IT'S WAR!!!

Little Redheaded Rosenthal and Big Bad Wolff to Face Off in Election of Condo President

by Marvin Luchman

Fireworks exploded at today's Condo Association meeting, as longtime Beau Mirage President Jobie Wolff was challenged in the upcoming election by political outsider Fern Rosenthal (Apartment 22-C). Wolff, who has served as president since she and her late husband, Saul, founded the Beau Mirage Board back in the pioneering days of the mid-eighties, announced that she would continue on "since obviously no one is crazy enough to take on this big pain in the tuchis." Rosenthal suddenly sprang to her feet and said, "I'm crazy enough!" Then she was nominated by her husband, Harry, who claimed, "I'm sure my wife will do as beautiful a job with this condo

Pain in the tuchis!
— *Jobie Wolff*

as she did with last year's Purim Carnival." His wife then told the sitting president to "Put that in your minutes, Mrs. Stalin!" Wolff, with a thunderous face, slammed down her gavel and exclaimed, "So let it be written, so let it be done!"

When asked for a comment after the meeting, Wolff said, "I will have to be dragged kicking and screaming from this office." "Jobie is the sort of person who needs to be involved," says friend Bella Weissman. "She would have been devastated when her husband Saul died if it wasn't for this job. As it was, she was so busy with the annual Canasta tournament that she almost missed his funeral." Hold onto your yarmulkes, ladies and gents, we're in for a Battle Royale!

I'm crazy enough!
—*Fern Rosenthal*

Mondo Condo

Beau Mirage News and Views

Special Edition Election Coverage

Special Edition Election Coverage

New, larger easy to read print　　　　　　**Week of October 14**

MIRAGE POLL

by Harold Ginsburg
Resident political analyst

With one week left until Beau Mirage residents vote on a new president, our survey shows that Fern Rosenthal holds a razor-thin lead over incumbent Jobie Wolff. Here's how the numbers break down.

Widows

Rosenthal	22%
Wolff	75%
Undecided	3%

Widows seem to associate with Wolff's loneliness.

Grandparents

Rosenthal	80%
Wolff	18%
Undecided	2%

Wolff banned unaccompanied grandchildren from the building last year when they pushed all the elevator buttons and the paramedics couldn't get up to resuscitate Mrs. Finkle, who was a widow. "There's a vote I lost," complains Wolff.

Neither candidate can count on the usually unreliable Alzheimer vote.

To Tag or Not to Tag, That Is the Question!

by Marvin Luchman

The battle lines have been drawn in the condo presidential elections. Current president Jobie Wolff, whose past accomplishments include the "Wild Duck Euthanasia Program" to clean up the lawns and "Oxygen Tank Recycling," says if elected, she will initiate a program of identification tags that all residents would be required to wear while using the pool and cabana area. Her challenger, the ever-quotable Fern Rosenthal, asked, "Aren't these tags reminiscent of another horrible dictator?" When questioned as to what burning issue was making her seek office, Rosenthal replied, "I hate Jobie's guts! I want to win so I can shove that gavel of hers right up her big fat Hungarian a-s!" Wolff declined comment on Rosenthal's remarks except to say that she was of Romanian descent.

RE-ELECT
JOBIE WOLF

"Everything is Coming Up ROSENTHAL"

Tags are for Dogs!!!

STOP THE PRESSES!!

Christie, our specialist from "Pool So Clean," quit today claiming that a male condo resident slapped her buttocks. An investigation has been launched.

Special Edition
Election Coverage

Mondo Condo

Beau Mirage News and Views

Special Edition
Election Coverage

New, larger easy to read print   **Week of October 21**

Scandal Rocks Election!!!!

by Marvin Luchman

Everything was going Fern Rosenthal's way as Beau Mirage residents gathered to hear the candidates and vote yesterday. During a rousing campaign speech Rosenthal said, "I know many of you will not make it to the next millennium, but if you vote for change tonight, you will be remembered as someone who made a difference!" She then challenged residents to get up and yell, "I'm mad as hell and I'm not going to take it anymore, tags are for dogs!" Those that could stood; others waved canes or stamped their walkers answering Rosenthal's rallying cry. Then Wolff sauntered up to the podium and silenced the crowd by asking, "How long have you known the Rosenthals? I've known them long enough to know that she cut down a Royal Palm Trcc because it was blocking the view from her bathroom window and he is a pervert!" Wolff then produced an enlarged picture of a "Rosenthal for President" sticker that she claimed had been slapped on the buttocks of Christie, our specialist from "Pools So Clean," by Mr. Rosenthal. Upon hearing this, Rosenthal charged at Wolff, screaming, "How dare you accuse my Harry of this, you frustrated old bitch!" The two candidates then became embroiled in a fist fight, the likes of which has not been seen here since the Mah-Jongg riots of 1992.

The two women were eventually separated by Mr. Rosenthal and Carlos the caterer, but not until $328.00 worth of damage had been done. A walnut veneer podium and the portable sound system

Sticker on Pool Girl's buttocks

were knocked over, leaving the card room in a shambles. Wolff, whose glasses were broken during the brouhaha, vowed to Rosenthal, "You'll be hearing from my optometrist!" Later the Rosenthal camp released a statement saying she was dropping out of the race to spend more time with her family, adding, "You won't have Fern Rosenthal to kick around anymore." Wolff was sworn into office an hour

Jobie Wolff and Fern Rosenthal

later by Rabbi Meyer Plotnick of Temple Beth Israel in an emotional ceremony at the shuffleboard courts.

Condo VOICES

Maybe if Mrs. Rosenthal spent more time in the bedroom,
her husband "Bob Packwood" could keep his hands to himself.
—*Jobie Wolff*

I got a novel idea for a sticker site!
Hasn't anyone got a sense of humor anymore?
—*Harry Rosenthal*

Harry Rosenthal once adjusted the brake on my wheelchair
and I caught him looking up my skirt.
—*Martha Kopplestien*

Next time I want to serve my community remind me what bastards they are.
—*Fern Rosenthal*

Trevor Ayliss
& Barrington LeTi
Willows Mews Co
Osterly on the G
Middlesex, MD12

(Come off the M40 at the Robin I

Mystery Man accompanies millionairess Mallory Blair.

Seen going into a restaurant called *La Traviata* was Mallory Blair the high profile millionairess, and a tall, dark, mystery man. Mrs. Blair the

TREVOR AYLISS
ON POLITICS

Dear Mam,

How about this photo in the paper of your jet-setting son, taken out-side a fancy Washington restaurant with a beautiful so-cialite? Don't worry, I haven't gone straight! You remember Mallory Blair, don't you? We used to work for Pan Am together in the early '80s. She's the one who met a ninety year old in First Class, mar-ried him pronto, and then he dies three months later, leaving her millions! (Every stewardess's dream.) You did meet her briefly at the Heathrow Christmas Party last year when we all danced to the "Spice Rack Girls," as you kept calling them.

Well, anyway, she called me at my stopover hotel last week and asked me if I'd act as the "beard," as she was having a secret affair with a very well-known American politician and they didn't want to arouse suspicion. (Being a "beard" means playing the gooseberry, Mam.)

I asked her if being a decoy date I'd have to act all butch. "Not if it's a strain, Trevor," she said. She's such a love. So, not one to turn down some posh nosh, I went along, and when we got out of the limo, all the paparazzi flocked round us, asking who I was and half blinding me with their flashbulbs. I felt like I was at the opening of a Planet Hollywood! (Cousin Lynn says you're getting one of these in Leeds soon.)

Well, we get sat down and Mallory points out Senator Randall Stevens, sitting at another table. You know the type, good head of hair, perma-tan. I wish I had half of what he's spent on his teeth. Ey, Mam, a bit like your heartthrob, Jock Ewing. I bet that's made you snap to attention. Ooh, yes—now she's interested, dear!

Well, it turns out Mallory's a bit more serious about him than I thought, and she starts telling me that they have to be so careful because one day he may run for president, and any breath of scandal may hurt him. I asked about his wife and she says, "Oh, Trevor, it's a loveless marriage" (that old chestnut). "She's always off caucusing." Caucusing's a political term, although I know it sounds like something Dad used to do in his vegetable patch. Well, the senator saunters over while we're sharing a white chocolate gateaux, drizzled with raspberry coulis (Mallory's still very weight conscious, even though the chucking up in the loo phase is over), gives me a bone-crushing handshake, and asks us to come to his hotel for a nightcap.

It was then that I remembered that I'd seen this fella in the news, talking about putting up a ten foot wall between the U.S. and Mexico. I told Mallory this when he left, but she said he'd been "quoted out of context." "Right," I said. "But when we have a drink in his suite, I'd better not ask him about his views on gays in the military!"

Well we had a good giggle, but I could tell she was besotted with him, Mam, she never looked at her late hubby like that, all doe-eyed and flushed, except in the last month when she was hauling him on and off that flippin commode.

So we went gallivanting off to his hotel. But forget the nightcaps, I wasn't even offered a mug of Ovaltine! Madam Mallory gets met at the door of the presidential suite by his nibs in a terry robe, and your son the gooseberry is escorted down in the freight elevator by Chet, a very dishy secret serviceman. Well, that was a bit of fun, I thought, even though I had shocking heartburn when I got back to the room. Thank God, Barry had packed the liver salts!

The next morning I'm woken bright and early by Mallory, telling me that my services were still required, and could I escort her to a reception that evening at the Belgian Embassy. Well, I was a bit worried about renting a tux on such short notice, but I know how you enjoyed that coach trip to Brussels, and I thought they might have some chocolate lying about worth pinching! So I agreed to go.

So we get there, me all trussed up in a rented monkey suit. I've always thought that men in dinner suits can look like one of two types: His Royal Highness Prince Philip, or the manager of the Asaldo Cinema on the Ilkley High Road—I unfortunately fall into the latter category.

Mallory was all bright and bushy-tailed, although the previous night's liaison had been cut a little short when loverboy was smuggled out at 4 A.M. in a laundry bin and helicoptered off to his home state to be photographed with flood victims. Very glamourous!

I made a bit of a fool of myself when the waiter asked us if we'd care for some "Salmon en croute canapés." "Oh, we *serve* these in First Class," I blurted out. "I mean . . . we were *served* these in First Class, only last week." I asked Mallory to slap both my wrists very soundly!

Then over comes the senator, and I braced myself for another bone-crushing shake. Bloody hell, Mam, it was like getting your hand caught in a Black and Decker vice! So we make a bit of small talk, and then he says, "Trevor, we still haven't had that golf game, what do you play off?" I said, "Grass, as a rule." Not a titter, Mam. Sometimes Americans have no sense of humour. "I'll see you on the links this weekend," he says, then he trolls off to "glad-hand a few folks" as he calls it, and I told Mallory she could count me out. The high life was wearing a bit thin now, Mam, and I had to be home by Saturday to let the double glaziers in to fit the patio doors, as Barry was off to Chichester with Patrick, his bridge partner, to compete in the semifinal of the Omar Sharif Classic.

She looked dead disappointed and reminded me that I still owed her for keeping quiet about my affair with Raoul the chorus boy from *Kiss of the Spider Woman*. Well, I felt a bit torn when she mentioned that, so I told her I'd think about it and popped to the bathroom.

While I was in there splashing my temples, Chet the secret serviceman comes in and starts checking all the cubicles. "Do you have to do that every time your boss spends a penny?" I asked him. "Sir, I don't want anyone overhearing what I've got to say," he said. "In the service we're not supposed to have opinions, or at any rate express them, but I happen to like Miss Blair, and Senator Stevens may well be the future president of this country, but the man is a scum-sucking, dick-licking, ass-grabbing, slimeball, sonovabitch, pissant, shitbird. . . . This is off the record, of course." Mam, you could have knocked me down with a feather! He told me that Old Smoothie had been cheating on his wife for years, in a box at the Kennedy Center, the fax room at the Library of Congress, a tractor tire at Camp David. There's a way to ruin an outfit!

Well, I got the picture, but Mallory had no idea, she was blinded by love. I asked Chet how the senator had gotten away with it for so long. "With the help of people like yourself, Mr. Ayliss," he said. Well, Mam, that remark certainly put me in my place. I suddenly felt cheap and used, and decided to put a stop to his shenanigans, like Aunt Gloria did when she went after that GI with Gran's kitchen scissors.

When I got back to the soiree Mallory launches right in with, "Trevor, the senator has asked us to dinner." "Oh, that's very kind," I said. "But I think we just want to be on our own tonight, don't we Mallory?" "We what?" she said, looking gob-smacked. "Have you forgotten, darling, it's our anniversary," I said. "I think a little candlelit dinner à deux is what's called for tonight." Well, if looks could kill! He stood there for a moment, and then he drags me to one side and says, "Listen you little airline faggot, this isn't in the script!" I was tempted to head butt him, I can tell you, but sticks and stones, eh, Mam. So I just stared back at him and growled all Sean Connery–like, "Put your balls on hiatus, cos tonight's not the night!"

Then I took Mallory home, and she fought me like a wildcat in the cab, kicking me in the shins with her Manolo Blahnik heels and calling Chet a liar. She's still not talking to me, but she might understand one day.

Now hold on, it's not quite the end of the story, Mam. Last week I was on the San Fran route, and who should be in 3A and B, but Mr. and *Mrs. Randall Stevens*. You should have seen his face when I offered him the champagne and orange juice combination! She was as nice as pie, although I can see why he fools around, she looked like the love child of Barbara Bush and John Major.

Well, I couldn't resist putting the boot in one more time, so I came back and told him to make his in-flight movie selections early to avoid disappointment. "May I suggest *Fatal Attraction, Disclosure,* or how about *An Affair to Remember?*" Talk about tongue in cheek. It was a very long flight for Casanova, and the extra Tabasco sauce Glenn and I put in his veal piccata kept him trotting up and down that aisle. Anyway, I'll sign off now. Hope this letter finds you "in the pink."

Love, (your political animal of a son)

Trevor
x x x x x x x x x
x x x x x x
x x x x
x x
x

CHAPTER TWELVE
MISCELLANEOUS

La Granger

820 Valley Star Dr .Sherman Oaks, CA 91423

Dear Candy,

I jotted down all this year's tax info that I could remember. Please fill in the rest, you know I've never been good with numbers. Remember what a fiasco it was when I played the math teacher on *Welcome Back Kotter*!

INCOME: <u>Infomercial</u> ($1,500 — $5,000)
         Also received Salad Shooter, valued at $19.95. Do I have to claim this?

       <u>Conan O'Brien Show</u>
         (Do they still pay if you get bumped?)

       <u>Family Spending Channel</u>
- Commission on the sale of Linda Granger Recovery Dolls. ($195)
- Insurance settlement for injuries incurred on the set.($22,000)

       <u>Filled in for Chubby Checkers</u> in *Grease* for 1 week. Please contact Chubby to collect $1,500.

Residuals from *VIP Lounge*
(Besides Poland, Bulgaria, and
Albania, is it running anywhere else?)

BUSINESS DEDUCTIONS:

TRAVEL:
Round-trip economy airfare to Phoenix
for Linda Granger memorabilia conven-
tion. ($275)

Round-trip economy airfare to Cheyenne
for my starring role in Wyoming's Center
of the Performing Arts production of
Driving Miss Daisy. ($450)
I think they're supposed to reimburse
for this. But don't push it, I'm up for
next year's production of *Shirley
Valentine*. (I don't do theater for the
money, I do it for the love!)

AUTOMOBILE:
Travel to and from Castings: 27,594 miles.
Travel to and from Filming: 98$\frac{1}{4}$ miles.

MEDICAL, BEAUTY, AND FASHION:
Paulo's of Sherman Oaks
Hair and Nail maintenance. ($6,300)
(Doesn't include tips.)

<u>Mr. Kenny's Haute Couture</u>
-    Black sequin gown for the Gay Icon
Awards. ($795)
-    Black sequin pantsuit for business
meetings and castings. ($450)

<u>Upgrade to "Soy-So-Soft Breast Implants"</u>
    (It's worth it, they're organic!)

<u>Wrinkle Resurfacing Treatment</u>
    At the LASOBLAST clinic. ($650)

<u>Burn cream</u> (see above) ($75)

<u>Collagen shots</u> ($250)
    To replenish what time has depleted.

<u>Rabies shot</u> ($55)
    From when that dog attacked me at the
People for Ethical Treatment of Animals
dinner.

<u>Phen-Fen</u> ($350)
    Prescribed by Dr. Gould.

<u>Phen-Fen</u> ($425)
    Prescribed by Dr. Wexler.

<u>Phen-Fen</u> ($392)
    Prescribed by Dr. Clement.

<u>PROMOTIONAL</u>:

      5,000 8 x 10 Glossy head shots. ($2,500)

      "La Granger" Billboard above the Boy's Town Disco in West Hollywood. ($2,700)

      500 Linda's Lucky Lips key chain/condom cases, for giveaways at the Disco's 20th anniversary party for *VIP Lounge*. ($250)

Candy, if everything looks okay could you be a real sweetie and forward this over to the accountant Artie, I don't have his address since he's been released.

XXOXO

P.S. Please enclose picture with tax return.

To Mitch and the entire gang at the IRS. Please deduct the cost of this picture! Ha, ha. Love, Linda.

CHIC'S CAB RULES

1. DON'T TOUCH THE DRIVER— OR I FUCKING KILL YOU!

2. DON'T MAKE MUSIC REQUESTS. I LISTEN TO CLASSIC DISCO RADIO— YOU LISTEN TO FUCKING CLASSIC DISCO RADIO!

3. DON'T TELL ME DIRECTIONS—I KNOW QUICKEST ROUTE, IF YOU DID YOU'D BE CAB DRIVER, FUCKFACE!

4. LUGGAGE
   A. IF IT DOESN'T FIT UNDER THE SEAT, IT BELONGS IN THE TRUNK!
   B. IF IT BELONGS IN THE TRUNK, IT'S TOO FUCKING HEAVY FOR ME TO CARRY!

5. DON'T TELL ME TO STEP ON IT! I KNOW YOU ARE IN A RUSH, SHITBAG! SO AM I! TO GET YOU OUT OF MY FUCKING CAB!

6. DON'T GIVE ME THAT FEMINIST BULLSHIT ABOUT THE GIRLIE PICTURES I HANG IN MY CAB! I LIKE PUSSY AND I'M PROUD OF IT!

7. HARLEM IS CLOSED AFTER 5 P.M.

8. OH YEAH! AND HAVE AS NICE A FUCKING DAY AS YOU CAN IN THIS CRAZY FUCKING CITY!

JOE'S LIQUOR LOCKER

Ruby Romaine's
List of Things to Do:

Drugstore:
1. Vick's inhaler and vapor rub.
2. Pall Mall cigarettes (2 cartons)
3. Cough syrup extra-strength
4. Douche pumps (special order)
5. Buddy's ritalin re-fill
6. ~~Quaaludes~~
+ anti-psychotic medication (generic).

Groceries:
1. Kool-aid (Kiwi Tropical Punch)
2. Oreos   + ~~Quaaludes~~
3. Pall Mall cigarettes (2 cartons)
4. Buddy's dinners:
   Swanson frozen Salisbury steak x4
   Peanut Butter + Salami
   Fluffer Nutter Marshmallow dessert spread
5. 3 1/2 lbs. chicken necks + feet
6. Farmer John's Lard
7. Toothpicks
8. Canned candied yams (extra-large)
9. Cat litter
10. Mothballs

JOE'S LIQUOR LOCKER

Bank:
Cash welfare check and Buddy's V.A. check.

Liquor Store:
Vladimir's All-American Vodka
(Giganto size with easy-pour handle)
Pall Mall cigarettes (2 cartons)
Steal more pens and pads for grocery lists.
Party clams (in brine)

+ ~~Quaaludes~~

Note to Self: Remind Buddy they stopped making quaaludes!

SUGGESTED FOR INCLUSION IN THE STEWARD'S HANDBOOK.

Submitted by Trevor Ayliss

"GOING TO MEET JESUS"
(What to do when a passenger dies midflight)

First rule: Don't move them. It's very upsetting for the other passengers if you're lugging a corpse along the gangway behind the dinner trolley. Puts them right off their chicken à la creme.

PUT EYESHADES ON
STOPS HIS EYES FROM POPPING OPEN
AND STARING ACCUSINGLY AT EVERYONE
WALKING PAST.

HEADPHONES
STOPS BUSYBODIES
ASKING HIM QUESTIONS.

SEATBELT
SECURE TIGHTLY TO STOP HIM FROM
BANGING OFF THE CEILING DURING TUR-
BULENCE.

SHOELACES
TIE TOGETHER TO STOP HIM
FROM TRIPPING PEOPLE IN THE AISLE
WHEN RIGOR MORTIS SETS IN.

NOTE: Dead passengers are nothing to be afraid of—they're very well be-haved, most of the time.

In case of emergency, the convention is at the Fresno Conference Center (615) 555-3425 ext. 223

Dear Nurse Branginella,

Below is a list of a typical day with Mother. Know that I am only a phone call away and if need be I'll be speeding down the freeway on my moped and home in a jiffy. I wouldn't normally be gone overnight, but it's a mandatory bank seminar on "How to explain to people that the new $100 bill is not Monopoly money."

MOTHER'S ROUTINE

6 a.m.   Wake Mother up and remove her catheter.

7 a.m.   She likes a little livener in her glucose.

8 a.m.   At about this time Mother likes to listen to 98.6 WPLK (All Polka Radio).

              If she says "I hate you, you're trying to kill me!" don't pay any attention, it means just the opposite.

9 a.m.   Time to give Mother her bath and shave her corns. The Hoist does look rather medieval but I assure you that it works. You may need to attach weights to yourself for extra leverage (for a woman who is bedridden, it's amazing that she weighs over 200 pounds).

10 a.m.   Time for Mother's Metamucil. Try giving her the fizzy peppermint flavour (her halitosis isn't getting any better), but she'll probably insist on her favourite, carob flavour.

11 a.m.	For elevenses Mother likes beef jerky, Triscuits, and Ovaltine liquidized with a splash of Lea & Perrins.
12:30 p.m.	Mother needs turning after her snack. I like to think of her as a large pot roast.
1 p.m.	Mother is usually pretty punctual using the potty. Don't throw it away because she likes to check her stool. She likes to do a texture test with a tongue depressor.
2 p.m.	Try and take Mother outside for her daily constitutional.
3 p.m.	Mother likes to go out shopping with her friends in the afternoons, so you'll get a couple of hours off. (Just kidding!!! Ha, ha.)

If you have to call the paramedics, don't let a young Mexican fellow called Victor come in. He came round once and Mother said he put his hand down her front. I think she was exaggerating, but she refuses to have him here.

Don't let Mother near the emergency button, she only uses it because she likes the sound of the siren on the roof going off.

If the lung machine starts making a "Humph, Humph" noise, unplug it and plug it back in again very quickly. If that doesn't do the trick, hit it 3 times with the mallet you'll find attached. Oh . . . it's all so complicated, maybe I shouldn't go. . . .

THE SECRET PAGES FROM JANIE PILLSWORTH'S CONTACT BOOK

Name / Nome / Nom: ~~Calvin Klein + Kelly Klein~~ **Address / Indirizzo / Addresse:** — (212) 555-6745 not important anymore **Telephone / Telefono / Téléphone:**	**Name / Nome / Nom:** Tiger Woods **Address / Indirizzo / Addresse:** — (212) 555-8374 Mobile in breast pocket of Nike shirt. No answer means he's putting. **Telephone / Telefono / Téléphone:**
Name / Nome / Nom: John Galliano **Address / Indirizzo / Addresse:** ~~Givenchy (Paris)~~ Christian Dior (Paris) "La Club Derriere" (Paris) **Telephone / Telefono / Téléphone:** — 01133 (23) 555-6454	**Name / Nome / Nom:** Colin Powell **Address / Indirizzo / Addresse:** e-mail@www. : .com **Telephone / Telefono / Téléphone:**
Name / Nome / Nom: J. D. Salinger's cellular **Address / Indirizzo / Addresse:** - ⟍·⊶⊣⊩ ⇄⇟ ⇟⇟⇟⊣ (Note to myself: don't ~~forget how to decode this.)~~ **Telephone / Telefono / Téléphone:**	**Name / Nome / Nom:** Chelsea Clinton **Address / Indirizzo / Addresse:** — Stanford ext.4746 Phone booth at top of dorm (only good after 2 a.m. and before 5 a.m.) **Telephone / Telefono / Téléphone:**
Name / Nome / Nom: Boris Yeltsin **Address / Indirizzo / Addresse:** — 01134 (22) 364-7463 The Vodka Hut on the corner of Gorky St. **Telephone / Telefono / Téléphone:** (he's incoherent after 3 p.m.)	**Name / Nome / Nom:** The Pope Vatican City **Address / Indirizzo / Addresse:** — (233) 555-7673 (If put on hold, you have to listen to horrible **Telephone / Telefono / Téléphone:** Hymn musak)

CHARACTER COSTUMES

Birdie

Chris

Erin

ERIN McCOLL   233

Hope

HOPE FINCH

H.R.H.

Kay

Virginia

Chic

Fern

Janie

Linda

MRS. NOH

SYDNEY

Trevor

Ruby

Rayleen